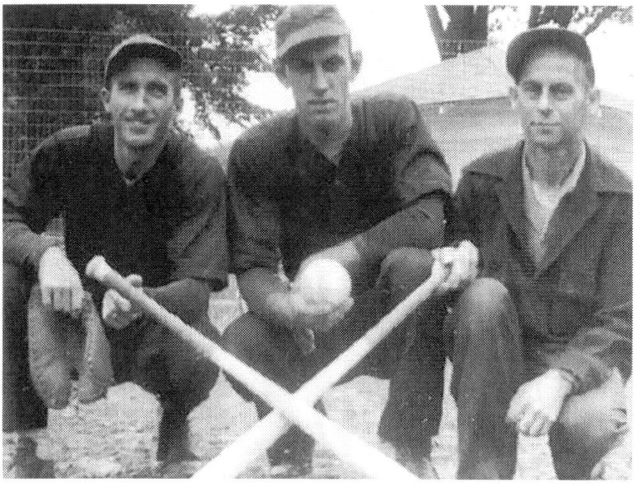

COUNTY'S LEADING WEEKLY
Durand Gazette

DURAND, ILLINOIS, THURSDAY, JULY 13, 1950

---

tributed a pair of singles.

Merchants 12, Rockford Palm Gardens 4

With Roy Wilke striking out thirteen and being found for only four hits, the Merchants put on their slugging clothes and roared away to a 12-4 nod over Rockford Palm Gardens, Sunday night.

The Locals, led by Lloyd Mulvain's three hits and Joe Hines home run and triple, rapped out ten safe blows in one of their heaviest displays of power shown this season.

Hine's home run with two on sparked a 5-run sixth inning which iced the game for the Merchants. His four-bagger, a line drive beyond the light pole in dead center field, was one of the hardest hit balls seen this year.

Merchants Record Now 16-5

The pair of wins upped the local's record to sixteen wins and five losses. Wilke's loss to the Playdiums was his first defeat in nine games.

Pete Adleman, Tip Tracy, Bump Sarver and Rollie Mulvain continue their commendable work as umpires, another thankless job, that of official scorer, has been capably handled by Abe Mulvain, Carl Nuss and Bump Sarver.

CARD OF THANKS

DURAND'S
Marvelous Merchants

A Tale of Small-Town Life
and Big-Time Softball

Mike Waller

All rights reserved
Copyright © 2018 Michael E. Waller
No part of this book may be reproduced, stored in a retrieval system or transmitted in any form or by any means, electronic, mechanical, photocopying, recording or otherwise, without the prior consent of Michael E. Waller.

Second Edition
ISBN 978-1727129694
Library of Congress Control Number: 2018910681

Designed and produced by Jean Donaldson Dodd

CreateSpace Independent Publishing Platform

Dust jacket illustrations: front, the Merchants at Legion Field; back, Roy Wilke.

CONTENTS

	Prologue	8
1	Build It, But Will They Come?	12
2	The Greatest Season	35
3	John R. Van Sickle's Durand Gazette	48
4	Running Out of Adjectives	63
5	A Lost Season	84
6	The Age of Innocence	101
7	Wilke's Swan Song	131
8	Start Slow, Fast Finish	143
9	Tragic Events	153
10	Whatever Happened to Them?	173

Acknowledgements ... 204
Notes ... 206
About the Author ... 213

"When I got the book, I said to myself, 'I care about the author, but why in the world would I care a thing about Durand and the Merchants?' Well, you made me care. It's a tender evocation of a delicious time when I was young and you were younger, and life — while not particularly easier — was a whole lot less complicated."

— *C. W. Gusewelle*
Former reporter and columnist, The Kansas City Star,
and author of a dozen books, including
The Rufus Chronicle: Another Autumn

For Roy Wilke

PROLOGUE

Two Funerals

The phone rang in the evening of Sunday, Feb. 13, 2005. It was my youngest brother, Steve Waller, with bad news. A neighbor had found our oldest brother, Dan, dead at age 68 on the kitchen floor in his home in Laurel, Md., where he had lived alone for 41 years. He obviously had been trying to reach the telephone when he died. Dan had been dead three or four days, possibly of a heart attack. He had lived more than 30 years with a brain tumor, so another suspect was a brain aneurysm. Our other brother, David, thought it might even have been a fatal mixture of medicine, which Dan had been taking most of his adult life. We never knew for sure since no autopsy was ever conducted.

Steve arranged for Dan's body to be flown back to Durand, our home town in Northern Illinois of 600 people that had grown in 45 years to 1,100. The visitation was held on Friday night, Feb. 18, at the McCorkle Funeral Home, which until a year earlier did double duty as a furniture store. It had been a marriage of commercial interests that was common in 19th Century America when furniture makers also built wooden coffins but was becoming rare in the 21st Century. The parlor is at 101 Main Street at the north end of the town square park.

More than 100 people paid their last respects, though Dan had not lived in the village since graduating from high school in 1956. He graduated in 1960 from the University of Wisconsin at Madison, served in the U.S. Army for two years and was an electrical engineer at the National Security Agency until retiring in 1995.

Among the mourners was Roy Wilke, our uncle. He and his wife, Judy, and our first cousin Jim Place and his wife, Sharon, walked through the receiving line together. I had not seen Roy since my father's funeral in February 1999. For the first time in my life, he looked his age, 79. In fact, he looked older, almost gaunt.

Roy said he, Judy and the Places were going to Davis, four miles west of Durand, for dinner after the visitation and would attend Dan's funeral the next day. A small crowd of family and friends gathered at St. Mary's Catholic Church for the funeral on Saturday and an even smaller group paraded in cars a half-mile to the church cemetery for burial after the services. But Roy and Judy were not there.

I talked to the Places the next day before returning to my home in South Carolina and learned that Roy had been coughing up blood the night after the visitation. A few days later he checked in with his physician at the Monroe, Wis., clinic, where doctors performed a series of tests. About a week later came the verdict: a cancerous tumor about the size of a hand had wrapped itself around Roy's liver. The prognosis, while unspoken, was gloomy.

Roy underwent a series of treatments in the next few months but doctors halted them when it became apparent it was too late. I phoned the editor of The Volunteer, Durand's weekly newspaper, to alert him to Roy's pending death. I told him that Roy had been the star pitcher on Durand's greatest fast-pitch softball team and that he might want to interview some surviving teammates to prepare an obituary.

A Midwestern cowboy and timber man all of his adult life, Roy and Judy and another couple took a 23-day car trip in late July to the American West to have one last look at the forests he so loved. He returned exhausted. Telephone conversations became impossible; death was closing in. Five weeks later, on Sept. 2, two days after his 80th birthday, he died.

I returned to Durand for services on Sept. 6 at McCorkle Funeral Home. The visitation was followed immediately by a Masonic ceremony and the funeral service, which opened with a song by Jerry Mulvain, Roy's outstanding catcher on the 1940s and 1950s softball team. The pastor of the Methodist Church invited guests to talk about Roy. A few responded, including me. I described Roy's unique pitching style which he called "the wheel," how he had loaned me money to help me go to college and his importance in my life. The services ended and many of us rode in the procession a mile up the hill past the Catholic and Lutheran churches for the burial in Durand Cemetery, adjacent to St. Mary's Cemetery.

We left the cemetery and returned to the town square to the

Masonic Hall, where we ate lunch. I sat with boyhood buddies Jim Walsh and Mike Mulvain and their wives, Cheryl Walsh and Pat Mulvain. The Mulvains 10 years earlier had bought a farm from Roy and turned it into a prosperous woodworking company. Joining us were Mike's uncle and aunt, Jerry and Juanita Mulvain. We talked about an hour about the great Merchants softball team. Mike, Jim and I reminisced about being members of the Foul Ball Brigade, risking life and limb running between parked cars at Legion Field to retrieve foul balls that were worth a nickel when turned in to the concession stand. We didn't know it at the time, but we were witnessing history in the making, watching perhaps the region's greatest small-town softball team as it feasted on the competition from the big cities of Rockford, Freeport and Beloit. Others sitting nearby seemed entranced by the stories. It became clear that few people knew or remembered much about those glory years and that little had been written about them.

A few days after returning to Hilton Head Island, the weekly Volunteer arrived in the mail. The obituary was a standard one, written in telegraphic style. The only reference to Roy's softball career were seven words: "Was pitcher for Durand Merchants Softball Team." It ended, "Roy wishes Everyone would plant a tree in his memory."

I debated with myself for the next several months about whether to attempt to write a book about the Merchants. Although the town's weekly newspaper of the era, the Durand Gazette, reported on the team, I knew the written record would be sketchy at best. Only three members of the original team still were alive. Without decent documentation, writing a book would be a pipe dream. But I didn't want the team's achievements or the joy of growing up in that era to be lost in time.

In late 2006, I phoned Bill Steward, who at 89 still lived in Durand where for 32 years he operated the town's barber shop. Steward loved baseball and the Merchants and reminisced about the team but was hazy about any details. He and his wife, Arlene, suggested I call Sherry McKenna Meinert, the writer of a history column in The Volunteer.

Sherry was immediately enthusiastic. She was delighted to search the newspaper clippings for any stories about the Merchants, since poring over clippings was a weekly requirement in writing her "Not So Long Ago..." column. Within two weeks a package arrived in the mail containing more than 100 clips about the Merchants from 1948 to 1955. While it was far from a complete record, it was enough for a good beginning. Thus was born "Durand's Marvelous Merchants: A Tale of Small-Town Life and Big-Time Softball."

Mike Waller, November 2007

PROLOGUE II

From left: Fred Geiser, Jerry Mulvain, Mike Waller, Ken Ditzler and Bernie Figi at a book-signing for Durand's Marvelous Merchants at the Durand State Bank in April 2008. (Photo by Mo Ostergard).

Shortly after Durand's Marvelous Merchants was published in November 2007, I began getting emails and letters from readers, some of whom had contributed to the book. Many of them also attended a book-signing event at the Durand State Bank, where they talked at length about life in the 1940s and 1950s.

Reading the book had jogged their memories. They remembered more stories that they hadn't mentioned in earlier interviews.

After hearing their new stories and reading all the new material it became clear that most of it belonged in the book. So years later, after writing two other books, I began revising the Merchants' book. Most of the additional material is in Chapter 1, which offers much more detail about the town businesses that sponsored the Merchants; Chapter 6, about what it was like growing up in a small town; and Chapter 10, about whatever happened to the ballplayers and important town figures. It also gave me the opportunity to add 15 photographs and make a few corrections in the original book.

I hope you think the Second Edition is an improved version of Durand's Marvelous Merchants.

Mike Waller, October 2018

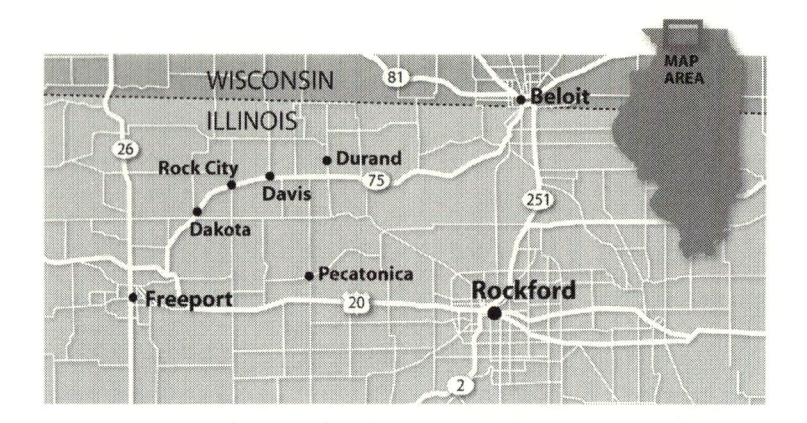

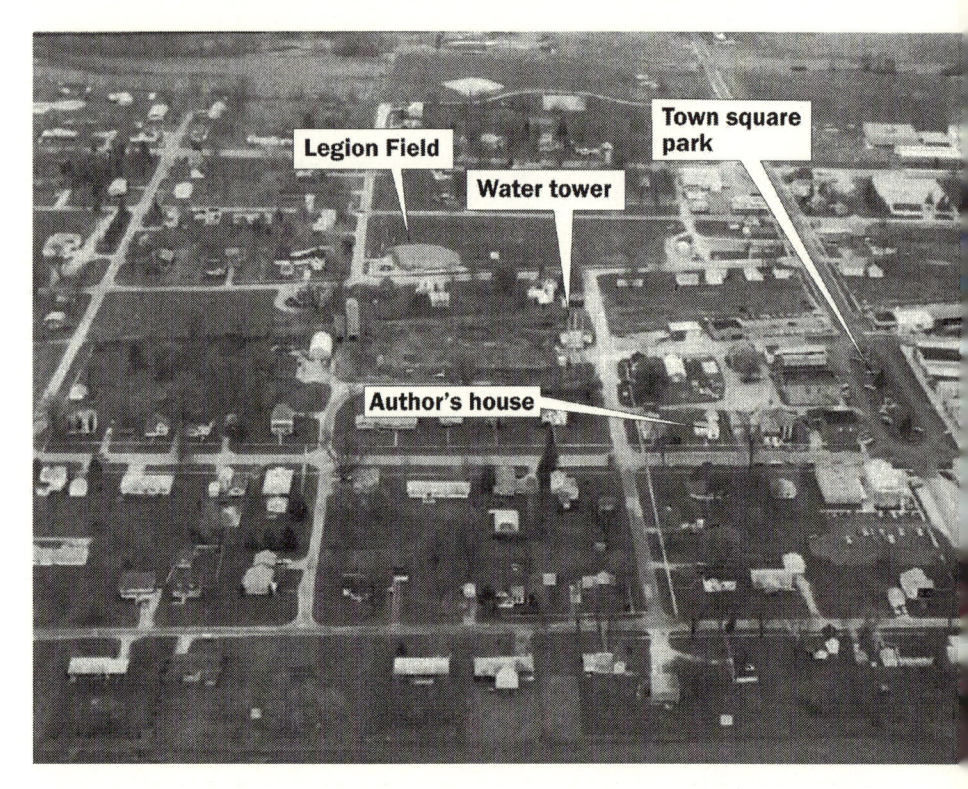

An aerial view of Durand, taken in the 1970s, showing the east side of the town looking south, with the town square park at right center. (Photo courtesy of Helen C. Johnson).

CHAPTER 1

Build It, But Will They Come?

Many of them were veterans of World War II, the young men who would form the first Durand Merchants fast-pitch softball team. They were members of what journalist Tom Brokaw called the Greatest Generation, surviving what the estimable British historian John Keegan called "the largest single event in human history, fought across six of the world's seven continents and all its oceans. It killed fifty million human beings, left hundreds of millions of others wounded in mind or body and materially devastated much of the heartland of civilization."

Of 171 Durand boys sent to the war, they were among the lucky ones, coming back alive, unlike seven who didn't. They returned from the war determined to carve out more peaceful and prosperous lives, start families and help revive the communities they had left. And play softball, a favorite sport of the era.

The World War II veterans on the 1948 roster included:

▶ Catcher Jerry Mulvain, age 22. He joined the Marines three months out of Durand High School in 1943 and served in the South Pacific, including during Gen. Douglas MacArthur's reconquest of Leyte Island in the Philippines in October 1944. Jerry worked for the local Highway Department.

▶ Shortstop Lloyd Mulvain, 28, the brother of Jerry and also a Marine. He was among thousands of American troops who battled the Japanese at Iwo Jima in February and March of 1945. Lloyd was a lineman for a gas and electric company.

▶ Second baseman Bob Highland, 28, who fought in Europe with the Army. He was wounded at Anzio beachhead in Italy and received the Purple Heart. He delivered oil and kept the books for a town service station and also owned a Durand grocery store with his wife and sister-in-law.

▶ Third baseman Wayne Adleman, 28. He joined the Navy in 1944 but was on a ship that never saw action in the war. He worked for a manufacturing company in Rockford, a city with a population of about 100,000 twenty miles southeast of Durand.

▶ Left fielder Fred Geiser, 20. He left Durand High School before his senior year after the war ended in 1945 and joined the Navy Seabees, serving for two years on a salvage crew in Japan and Southeast Asia. He was a farmer.

▶ Right fielder Keith "Bud" Smith, 26, who shared the position with several players, including his younger brother George. Bud was in the Army Transportation Corps in France during the war. He worked for a manufacturing company in Rockford.

▶ Right fielder George Smith, 24. He saw action with the Army Medical Corps in Southeast Asia. He worked for a Rockford manufacturing company.

▶ Outfielder Wayne "Red" Barron, 24, who also pitched and played first base. He served in the Army in France and Germany and was wounded in the Battle of the Bulge, receiving the Purple Heart. He also worked for a Rockford manufacturing company.

The World War II veterans were joined by four other players:

▶ First baseman Dick Highland, 27, Bob Highland's younger brother. He owned and operated a feed store in the village.

▶ Center fielder Joe Hines, 23, who owned and operated a farm four miles north of Durand.

▶ Right fielder Jack Yaun, 23, who served in the Korean War. He was a farmer.

▶ Pitcher Roy Wilke, 22, the heart of the team. He was a cattle rancher and timber buyer for a woodworking company.

All of the players attended Durand High School except for the Highland brothers, graduates of Pecatonica High School, and Wilke, a graduate of Dakota High School.

From 1946 through most of the summer of 1948, some of them played on the Durand Town Team or the Irish Grove team at Rock City, a town of about 150 people seven miles west of Durand. Softball was the main form of summer recreation for young adults as well as teenagers. It also provided the chief entertainment each week for fans, who gathered in Rock City several times a week to watch dozens of teams play in the Rock City league. Teams from all over Northern Illinois and Southern Wisconsin played in Rock City because it had one of the few lighted ball diamonds in the area. It was built in 1935 with lights that had been used at the Chicago World's Fair of 1933-1934.

The diamond was constructed on land in the business district where about one-fourth of the downtown buildings were destroyed in a fire on April 6, 1927. Many ball players recalled sliding into second base and seeing pieces of glass or old nails that had worked their way to the surface. The outfield was slightly uphill and a road ran through the back of it. A long fly ball meant a race across the road to catch it. It was not a perfect ball diamond, but it was the best lighted field of its time in the area.

The Durand Gazette published every Thursday but rarely covered the games in those early years. An exception appeared on May 30, 1946, when the paper printed a two-paragraph account on Page One (all softball stories always were published on Page One) of the opening game of the Rock City night softball league. Wilke, the only player mentioned, pitched a two-hitter and the Durand Town Team shut out Rock Grove 13-0. Another rare story, one paragraph, appeared on June 20, 1946, heralding Durand's unbeaten record after defeating Dakota 14-5.

The paper didn't publish any accounts of games in 1947 and only a handful in 1948. The first story appeared on June 17, citing a 14-13 come-from-behind victory by Durand a week earlier over Dakota. A week later Rock City massacred Durand 23-3. The story included no names but, surely, Wilke did not pitch in such a one-sided losing effort. By early July, the league standings in the first half of the season were:

	W	L
Rock City	4	2
Durand	4	2
Dakota	3	2
Cedarville	3	3
Irish Grove	0	5

As the town team played in the summer of 1948, efforts were already underway to build a new lighted ball diamond in Durand at the corner of Dayton and East Elm Street, about a four-minute walk from my home on East Main Street. While Durand's streets had names, none of us knew them because street signs weren't erected until after I left for college in 1959.

The ballpark campaign was led by the American Legion Gold Star Post 676 and two of its members, George Smith and Dr. T. H. "Doc" Young. Smith was a part-time right fielder who entered the Army after graduating from Durand High School in 1943. He was assigned to the Medical Corps and served for 20 months in China, Burma and India.

He was discharged in February 1946 and worked at several jobs, including as a fireman at Camp Grant in Rockford and a carpenter. He joined the Woodward Governor Co. in Rockford as a machinist in February 1947.

Doc Young — the T stood for Thomas but everyone called him Doc — was a native of Rock City, went to high school in Savanna, Ill., and graduated from the Chicago College of Dental Surgery in 1910. He opened his practice the same year in Durand and fell in love with the village. To say Doc was a character was like saying Joe DiMaggio could hit.

"I'll take small-town dental practice any day," Doc told The Freeport Journal-Standard in an interview for a story on March 17, 1960, highlighting his 50 years as a dentist and civic leader. "I know a lot of big city dentists who wear neatly pressed trousers and nicely shined shoes but have dirty underwear. A dentist has a lot of expensive social obligations in a larger city that you don't have in a small town. Then, too, you can't beat the friendliness of a town like Durand."

And friendly it was to a man of Doc's leadership talent. If it needed doing, Doc did it. He organized the first Scout troop in March 1923, a few years after serving in the Army Medical Corps during World War I and helping found Durand's American Legion Gold Star Post 676 in August 1920. For several summers he took the time to oversee a Scout camp for Durand boys. By the mid-1920s, he had become very concerned about fire protection in the town.

In the early 20th Century, fires had ravaged much of Durand's downtown district. Two years after Doc arrived in town, a fire that started in the Geary Restaurant destroyed it, Randall and Hartman's Meat Market, F.L. Randall's pool hall, the Mylott and Van Sickle's harness shop and Mrs. G. P. Crowder's millenary store, the second floor of which housed the offices of Doc and Dr. C. A. Roberts. The town's fire engine, as usual, was out of commission so a bucket brigade was formed. But it could do little; the fire actually was stopped by a stone building housing B. P. Morey's grocery store.

Thirteen years later, fires burst out again. On Nov. 7, 1925, the hardware store at the north end of town square park that had just been bought by Floyd "Bill" Hartman and Frank "Ted" Haggerty from J. C. Van Sickle went up in flames. High wind swept the blaze to the Methodist Church on the north and to Dr. Lins' office on the east. The heat was so great that the bucket brigade was ineffective. A call for help to the Rockford fire station 17 miles east saved the day. Forty men in fire trucks arrived 45 minutes later driving through deep snow. They brought the fire under control but not before all the buildings, plus the second floor of Mae Crowder's home east of the church, were destroyed.

Doc Young came to the rescue. He organized and led the campaign in 1926 to build and formally register a fire department in Durand. His efforts resulted in Durand creating the first volunteer fire protection district in Illinois — the Winnebago County Fire Protection District #1, a taxing body similar to a school district. "We set up an imaginary circle around Durand with a radius of six miles," he said. "We raised $7,000 by subscription to buy necessary fire-fighting equipment and held dances and other social functions afterward to raise other needed money."

Local response was mostly favorable, but there was some opposition. That didn't deter Doc. "Some of the farmers who refused to contribute any money toward the equipment were the very ones whose farms we saved a couple of years later. We fixed them, though. They got a bill for it while others didn't."

Doc became the new department's first fire chief and then headed another campaign that led to the installation in 1928 of a new waterworks system and water tower near the stockyards, a stone's throw from my backyard. He then became the resident engineer for the system. In the same year, the town erected a combination town hall and fire station a half-block west of the town square park on the south side of East Howard Street. The fire siren sat atop this building and was activated by the telephone operator who then plugged in the fire phone and sat with the key open, disregarding all other calls, until the first fireman to reach the station barked "Where's it at?" and she could tell him the location and nature of the blaze. During World War II, Doc was a member of the Winnebago County Selective Service Board, a position he held for 25 years.

In his younger days, Doc had been a cracker jack of a catcher on the Durand baseball team, according to some old-timers. So it wasn't any surprise that he would join Smith to lead the effort to build the Legion Memorial Field.

They had plenty of help. Orville Keller acquired in April 1948 for $180 the property (formerly known as the Morris property) and the abandoned house on it known as the Ritter house, a favorite but outlawed and thought-to-be dangerous playground of many of us boys. Keller then donated the property to the Legion. The house was condemned and volunteers, led by Smith and the Mulvain brothers and including ball players as well as many other town folks, flocked to the field to start the clean-up. Carl Holland, who worked for the Winnebago County Highway Department, brought in the county's Caterpillar on Memorial Day weekend and began the job of clearing the land. Dozens of area farmers, including outfielders Fred Geiser, Joe Hines and Jack

Yaun, brought in machinery daily, razing the house and dozens of trees. Those that couldn't be bulldozed were dynamited. The Mulvains' father, Lawrence, had access to dynamite. He and others bored under the center of the trees and buried the charges deep to avoid pelting the area with clumps of dirt, which happened to some degree anyway. Some of the trees had to be dynamited more than once. Still, a few defied the blasts and continued to stand strong and tall. Workers stood in the deep holes below the strongest and finally toppled the trees by cutting their roots with chain saws. The project was a tremendous community effort.

As the ball diamond began to take shape, the Gazette published a story on Aug. 5, 1948, at the top of Page One that announced the need for volunteers:

> "Volunteer help is needed to prepare the Legion ball diamond for use. Volunteers will gather at the new ballpark this Thursday and Friday evening to rake and clean the diamond.
>
> "All interested workers are asked to bring rakes and shovels and be on hand one or both of these evenings.
>
> "The lights have arrived for the park. As soon as the poles can be placed and the lights installed, the boys will begin using the diamond."

The Charge of the Light Brigade was led by Francis "June" Amundsen, Lloyd Mulvain, Paul Downing and Smith. Amundsen, my godfather and a Marine who like Mulvain served on Iwo Jima and in the South Pacific during World War II, was a foreman on electrical line construction for the L.E. Myers Co. of Rockford. Mulvain was a lineman for the Central Illinois Gas & Electric Co. also working out of Rockford. Downing also worked for Central Illinois Gas. They got lots of help from other volunteers.

A three-day local carnival raised $1,060 for the ballpark, of which $746 was spent on 24 1,500-watt lights. Amundsen, who got the light poles at a discount from his company, was chief of the installation crew. Lionel "Curley" Weaver, an Army Air Force veteran, was in the electrical wholesale business and got a deal on the ballpark lights. The Light Brigade, working several long days, finished its work in less than one week.

The town team continued its competition in the Rock City League. On Aug. 12, the Gazette for the first time referred to the team as the Durand Merchants as it clung to first place with two victories. They defeated Rock City 7-6 on Friday, Aug. 6, and beat Cedarville 10-5 on a three-hitter by Wilke on Monday, Aug. 9. They had lost only one game in the second half of the season.

The four-paragraph story ended with an update on the progress at Legion Memorial Field:

> "Work on the new ball diamond at Durand is progressing rapidly. The poles and lights are in place and the lights should be adjusted this week. It looks now like the cry of 'play ball' will be heard on the new Legion ball diamond sometime next week."

The prediction was optimistic. The Merchants played in Rock City the next week, defeating Dakota 15-5 to remain in first place.

Finally, on Sept. 2, 1948, the newspaper announced the opening of the new ballpark in a four-inch story, long by Gazette standards:

> "For months plans and preparations have been underway for the new Legion Memorial ballpark diamond. Hours and hours of labor have gone into the project.
>
> "But, tonight is the night that all have been awaiting — the grand opening of the new diamond with two ball games.
>
> "The Durand Cub Scouts will tackle Davis, while the main attraction will be the game between Durand and Rock City.
>
> "The members of the local Legion post wish to take this opportunity of saying thank you to the many persons who have helped in any way to make this project a success.
>
> "Financial support for the new lighted ball diamond was received from the carnival, a trap shoot staged by the Sportsman's club, a

combined dance of the Legion and New England Grange, and from donations given by several organizations.

"The many hours of actual labor donated is appreciated very much.

"The Legion members hope that the park will be of great benefit to the youth and adults of our community.

"Be sure to attend the opening games tonight. Refreshments will be on sale. This has been made possible by parents of the scouts."

The story of the opening of the Legion Field was not the only big news of the week. An item in the next column announced the wedding at the Methodist Church of the principal of the Durand Grade School, Dorothy Johnson, to the town's physician, Dr. Isadore Schwartz. Miss Johnson was the daughter of Mr. and Mrs. Elmer Johnson and had received her bachelor of education degree earlier in 1948 from DeKalb State Teachers College, now known as Northern Illinois University, about 50 miles southeast of Durand. Dr. Schwartz did graduate work at George Washington University in Washington, D. C. and at the University of Wisconsin at Madison. He had been practicing medicine in Durand since November 1946.

After heralding the opening of the new ballpark for several weeks, the Gazette's Sept. 9 account of the first game was a huge disappointment. It was only three paragraphs — one of those announcing next week's game — under a small headline reading "OPEN NEW DIAMOND" and mentioned the game as an afterthought:

"A large crowd was on hand for the opening of the Legion Memorial ball diamond last Thursday night.

"A total of $73 was collected as a free will offering from the spectators. In addition the scouts turned in about $20 that they made on ice cream and cake. All of this money went to the ballpark fund. Durand defeated Rock City 3-2 in the softball game.

"The Durand Merchants will play the I. A. Myers team from Rockford tonight at the new ball diamond. The game will start at 8 p.m."

It would not be the only time that the Gazette's news judgment was daffy.

Another story in the next column, with a much larger headline reading "Benefit Game For Highland," reported on another Merchants' victory at the Legion Field that week:

"A friend in need is a friend indeed.

"Bob Highland knows that this old adage is very true. The Durand boys played Irish Grove at the new diamond Monday night in a benefit ball game for him.

"The local team collected $117 for Bob and won the game in addition, 11-2.

"Bob had played with the team all summer, until he recently underwent surgery.

" 'I want to thank the members of the team and everyone who contributed to the fund,' declared Bob as he stopped at the Gazette office Tuesday."

What the story didn't mention was that Highland had broken his ankle in a Merchants' game a few weeks earlier when a player on the opposing team — no one remembers which team — slid hard into him at second base. Many Merchants thought it was a brazen attempt to injure Highland and a fight among players nearly erupted. Highland, an excellent second baseman, would never play with the Merchants again.

The account also was the only time in the Merchants' era that a ballplayer was quoted in a Gazette story, common by today's sports reporting standards but rare in all newspapers in the 1940s and 1950s. And it was the last game story published in the Gazette in 1948.

The Sept. 9 edition also reported the grade school opened with 152 students enrolled. It listed the 28 first graders, at the time the largest first-grade class in Durand history: Gary Tracy, William Keller, Alan Norsworthy, Lynn and Lyle Clark, Marsden Patterson, Shirley Adleman, Bonnie Selden, James Spelman, Patty Madonna, James Walsh, Joyce Kinney, Shirley Morgan, Shirl Fostler, Fred Harris, Eugene Laube, Carol Highbarger, Arthur Nath, David McCartney, Maurice Ostergard, Michael Mulvain, Dannie and Donnie Carter, Billy Harris, Barbara Haughton, Jimmie Harrole, Shirley Ritter and Sharon Buffington. I was a year ahead of them, in second grade.

The last Gazette story mentioning the new ball diamond in 1948 appeared on Oct. 21 and reported that bleachers and a concession stand would be constructed before the 1949 season opened. It also thanked Durand businessmen who donated a total of $365 to the park. It elaborated: "This money will be used to pay for the light poles and help defray other expenses. There still remains $250 to be paid. Anyone who wishes to make a donation may do so by contacting Lloyd." Lloyd, of course, was Lloyd Mulvain, the shortstop and chairman of the Legion's baseball committee.

Several businesses — the merchants of Durand, from which the team got its name — contributed to and sponsored the team. Most of them surrounded the town square park that was about a football field long and 25 yards wide. The businesses included:

▶ The Durand Service & Equipment Co., the Chevrolet and John Deer dealership at 428 Center Street owned by Frank "Ted" Haggerty and John Walsh. They had purchased the old Randall property at the northwest corner of Center Street. They tore down all three of the buildings on the property and erected a large, new structure. Haggerty, Walsh and Jim Slocum formed the company in 1945 and originally sold Plymouth and DeSoto automobiles. Slocum sold Haggerty and Walsh his interest in the business in February 1949 and acquired their interest in the Durand Service Station, making him the sole proprietor of the Smith Oil and Refining Co. station. Haggerty and Walsh then acquired the John Deere and Chevrolet dealerships and also sold DeLaval products. The dealership prospered until 1964, when Haggerty and Walsh leased the building to Durand Precision Products, created by three businessmen including Robert H. Spengler, a Rockford industrialist. The building now houses McCorkle's Furniture Store.

► Doty Motors at 400 Center Street on the southwest corner of Center and Howard streets and Spelman Implement across the street at 101 West Howard, the Ford auto and tractor dealership owned by Rod Doty and Leo Spelman. Doty and Spelman were partners in Durand's Diamond Oil Station when Spelman married Allene Leech on Feb. 12, 1934. The station at the northeast corner of Center Street and East Oak was so small that the grease pit was outside the building, next to Bliss Grocery, and if you weren't careful you could fall into it. In 1936, the partners obtained the Ford dealership for Ford cars and trucks. Seven years later Doty and Spelman purchased the two Shorb buildings at the corner of Howard and Center streets for their auto and tractor dealership. The corner building had been occupied by the Guse Tavern and the other building had been used by Graham Supply Co. for feed storage. Within weeks of the purchase, Doty was inducted into the U.S. Navy but the firm continued on as usual. In November 1946, after Doty was discharged, they opened their new Firestone store in the first store south of the Gazette's printing office on the west side of Town Square. In October 1953 they dissolved their partnership, with Spelman owning the implement company and DX station and Doty establishing his new business as Doty Motors. The Ford site is now owned by Bryden Ford and the Spelman building until a couple of years ago was a banquet hall operated by Hello Folks Restaurant.

► Bentley and Highland Grocery at 412 Center Street on the west side of Town Square Park owned by Ramona Bentley and her brother-in-law and sister, Bob and Margaret Highland. The grocery was operated for years by Dale Shakey, who purchased it in 1933 from Gerald Patterson. Shakey sold it to Bentley and Highland in the late 1940s and it discontinued operating in April 1962 after Ramona suffered an injury and could no longer work. The building then became a tavern.

► Bliss Grocery at 403 Center Street, across the street from Bentley and Highland Grocery, owned for 40 years by Gladys and Raymond Bliss. Gladys and her twin sister, Grace Thoren, began to work in the store in 1928. The twins graduated from the University of Illinois in 1931, returned to Durand and bought the store from Al Deal. Deal took over the business about six months later but after Gladys married Raymond Bliss Deal sold it again to the newlyweds. Another sister, Tressa Andrews, worked at the grocery store for several years. When Gladys took over the store, eggs sold for five cents a dozen and many people didn't have money. "We gave a lot of credit," Gladys recalled. "People were honest and they would pay. Kids didn't steal." Over the years, Gladys became a leading citizen. She was instrumental in the establishment of the Volunteer Fire Department (she and Grace donated an ambulance to the department in 1975), the Durand State Bank in 1957 and the Durand Medical Clinic shortly thereafter. She and my dad, Ward Waller, were named the town's first Citizens of the Year in 1976. The grocery store is now home to an insurance agency.

▶ Chapin's Furniture and Funeral Home at 101 West Main Street at the northwest end of town square park owned by Floy Chapin. She took over the firm after her husband Harry died in 1947, 10 years after erecting a new building at the site. Harry, from Rock Falls, had purchased the business in 1931 from J.M. Geary, who had owned it since 1899. Geary, Durand's oldest businessman at the time, told The Durand Gazette when he sold the funeral home, "I venture to say I have been in every house in the entire community." Floy, like Gladys Bliss, became a leading Durand citizen, helping establish the Durand State Bank. The Chapin business is now McCorkle's Funeral Home.

▶ Greene and McCarthy Implement Co., the Allis Chalmers franchise one mile south of town at the southeast intersection of Illinois Routes 70 and 75, owned by Charlie Greene and Al McCartney. McCartney bought out Greene in 1961. The franchise, now run and operated by his sons, Woody and Dave McCartney, and grandsons Jim, Mark and Andy McCartney, still operates at the same location as well as at several other locations in Illinois. It has the distinction of being Durand's oldest business. Al died at age 96 in December 2015.

▶ Durand Standard Service station at the northeast corner of Illinois Routes 70 and 75 across the road from Greene and McCartney.

The station was opened by George Stauffer and his son, Howard, in July 1932. A few years later Al Basse purchased it. In 1943, Greene bought the station and took on McCartney as a partner in 1948. They sold it in 1950 to Louis Thomas and Dick Highland, the Merchants' first baseman. After Highland's early retirement from the Merchants, he bought Durand Feed and Seed, which he sold in 1964 to the Winnebago Service Co. The gas station site is now a vacant lot.

► The Gulf Oil Service station at 423 Center Street across the park from the Chevrolet dealership. It was owned by Jim Slocum, who at one time was in partnership with John Walsh and Ted Haggerty but took over as sole owner in 1949. The station was next to the Yale Building, whose brick wall served as a great target to throw rubber baseballs against and take infield (ground ball) practice on Sunday afternoons when the station was closed. The site is now a vacant lot and the brick wall is home to a gigantic colorful mural celebrating Durand history

► The Durand Cheese Factory at 101 East South Street owned by Joe Buerkle and his son Joe Jr. Buerkle, of Brodhead, Wis., had purchased the site of the old Durand Seminary, which fronted Illinois 70, and put the finishing touches on the new $50,000 building in October 1941, when large crowds gathered for its opening. Buerkle, his wife and four children lived in the apartment above the factory, which was the first business a driver encountered once entering the city limits from the south.

► The Ploetz Pharmacy in the I. O. O. F. Building on the west side of the town square. Bill Ploetz bought the drug store in 1915 from C. A. Starr and operated it until he retired in 1956.

► Axel Erickson Clothing Store on the east side of the town square. Erickson arrived in Durand in 1899 and went to work for Albert Anderson, a tailor. In 1903 Erickson bought the store and started a men's furnishing business, which he operated for more than 50 years until he died in 1955.

► The Durand Bowl. The four-lane bowling alley was built in 1943 on the west side of the town square by Pete Adleman, the home plate umpire for the Merchants' games. The bowling alley had many different owners over the next several decades, including Fred Kranish, Melvin "Dutch" Hausvick, Russ Sarver and Durand High School basketball star Larry Damon.

▶ The Durand Barber Shop at 418 Center Street operated from 1947 to 1979 by Bill Steward. In about 1950, he bought the shop, located next to the Masonic Hall, which was erected in 1932, from Ellis Andrews, who purchased it in 1916 from T. R. Mahan.

▶ The Barker Lumber Co. of Delavan, Wis., which purchased the Durand Lumber Co. in 1925 and at one time operated eight other lumber yards in Northern Illinois and Southern Wisconsin.

▶ Tracy Tin Shop at 417 Center Street, operated at the back of the building on the east side of the park by Merchants' manager Chuck Tracy and his brother, Clifford "Tip" Tracy, from 1946 to 1961. The front of the building housed Viola's Beauty Shop, owned and operated by Viola Reed. In 1961 the Tracys moved their tin shop across the park to 414 Center Street, replacing the Post Office, which had operated there since the merged Citizen Bank and Durand State Bank closed in 1933 during the Depression.

▶ The Charles A. Miller Co. at 119 Oak Street, the burial vault manufacturing firm owned by Charlie Miller.

▶ The Durand Electric Service at 407 Center Street, operated by Robert LaGaisse from 1949 to about 1966.

▶ Durand Plumbing and Heating at 109 East Main, owned and operated by Artie Perkins and the Slamp brothers, Harold and Dwight. The building was a long putt from our house on East Main.

▶ T. H. Young and Victor C. Frame, the town dentists with offices on the second floor of the Yale Building at 425-427 Center Street next to the Gulf service station. Doc Young practiced in that office from 1912 to 1965.

The year's biggest news came in November when Harry S Truman was elected president in his own right by upsetting New York's Republican Gov. Thomas E. Dewey despite The Chicago Tribune claiming otherwise in a banner headline. The Chicago Cubs, the favorite team of most Durand baseball fans, once again finished in last place in the National

League with a 64-90 record, then a franchise record for futility. Rookie left-handed pitcher Dutch McCall set a Cub record with 13 consecutive losses. The Cubs' futility prompted owner Phil Wrigley to purchase in August full-page advertisements in all the Chicago newspapers apologizing to the fans. In the World Series, the Cleveland Indians — led by shortstop-manager Lou Boudreau, outfielder Lary Doby, the American League's first black player, and pitcher Bob Lemon — defeated the Boston Braves with its pitching mantra of "Spahn and Sain and pray for rain" four games to two. The two games won by the Braves were the victories of Warren Spahn and Johnny Sain, Boston's only reliable starting pitchers. The Rockford Peaches, members of the All-American Girls Professional Baseball League since its founding by Wrigley in 1943 when major league baseball suffered with so many of its players in the service, finished third in the 10-team league with a 74-49 record and won the playoff championship. Few people realize that when the league began the girls didn't play baseball. They played underhand fast-pitch softball with a ball 12 inches in circumference because none of them knew how to play baseball. Only after the war had ended did they switch to baseball.

The Merchants' season was a successful one and perhaps a championship one, though you couldn't tell by reading the Gazette. It never reported whether the Merchants won the Rock City League or on their record for the season. The town was buzzing in anticipation of next year's first full season at the new ballpark. The talk at Bill the Barber's shop was that the Merchants would be even better. The question was: Would they draw the kind of large crowds that would make the Legion diamond a field of dreams?

Dave Mulvain, left, age 8, and his brother, Mike, age 6, use their dad's (Lloyd Mulvain's) lineman equipment to climb the newly erected light poles at Legion Memorial Field in September 1948. (Photo courtesy of Dave Mulvain).

Paul Downing, in driver's seat, and Lionel "Curley" Weaver take a break during construction of Legion Field in September 1948. Weaver was in the electrical wholesale business and purchased the lights for the Legion at a discount. Downing worked with Lloyd Mulvain at the Central Illinois Gas & Electric Co. (Photo courtesy of Dave Mulvain).

Legion Field as it looked 10 years after being built. The view at home plate is looking northwest at the home team bench and bleachers during a Pony League baseball game. (Photo courtesy of Dave Mulvain).

Legion Field in 1958, with the view at home plate looking southeast at the visitors' bench. (Photo courtesy of Dave Mulvain).

Lloyd Mulvain in about 1950 warms up for a baseball game for Roper's, a Rockford team. (Photo courtesy of Dave Mulvain).

BUILD IT, BUT WILL THEY COME? 31

Durand's Center Street town square park in the mid-1940s. The view is looking at the east side of the square. Doc Young's dental office was in the second floor of the brick building on the far left, next to Jim Slocum's Gulf Oil service station. On Thursday nights during the summers, a sheet was tied to the two elm trees on the right and became the movie screen for the "free show." (Photo courtesy of Mo Ostergard and Dennis Bliss).

The World War I veterans' memorial at the south end of the Center Street town square park in the late 1940s. Huge elm trees lined the park. Visible on the left is the Chevrolet dealership owned by John Walsh and Frank "Ted" Haggerty. (Photos courtesy of Mo Ostergard and Dennis Bliss).

Gladys Bliss stands in front of the DX station in September 1944. The station was a popular hangout for teenaged boys in the 1950s. Gladys and my dad, Ward Waller, were the first to be named Durand's Citizen of the Year, in 1976. (Photo courtesy of Mo Ostergard and Dennis Bliss).

DURAND'S MARVELOUS MERCHANTS

The west side of the Center Street town square park facing north in the 1970s. Gone are the huge elm trees, not just at the park but all over Durand, killed by Dutch elm disease. McCorkle's Furniture and Funeral Home, formerly the Chapin Furniture and Funeral Home, is in the middle at the north end of Center Street. (Photo courtesy of Mo Ostergard and Dennis Bliss).

Bliss' Grocery, at the southeast corner of the Center Street town square park, in the mid-1940s. It was owned for 40 years by Raymond and Gladys Bliss. Next to it is the DX service station owned by Leo Spelman and Rod Doty. (Photo courtesy of Mo Ostergard and Dennis Bliss, youngest son of Raymond and Gladys Bliss).

The west side of the Center Street town square park in April 1944. The bowling alley on the left was built a year earlier by Earl "Pete" Adleman, who was the home plate umpire at most of the Merchants' games. Next to the bowling alley is Dale Shakey's Grocery. By the late 1940s it had become Bentley and Highland Grocery, owned by Ramona Bentley and her sister and brother-in-law, Margaret and Bob Highland, the team's second baseman who broke his ankle in a game in 1948 and never played again. (Photo courtesy of Mo Ostergard and Dennis Bliss).

A closer look at the bowling alley in October 1944, with its new neon sign. "It is colored and looms up like a million dollars at night," said Gladys Bliss. (Photo courtesy of Mo Ostergard and Dennis Bliss).

BUILD IT, BUT WILL THEY COME?

The four-lane bowling alley built in 1943 by Earl "Pete" Adleman, the home-plate umpire for most Merchant games. He sold it to Fred Kranish of Rockford in 1946.

CHAPTER 2

The Greatest Season

"Nobody goes there anymore, it's too crowded." — Yogi Berra

The great New York Yankee catcher Yogi Berra said that about Ruggeri's Restaurant in St. Louis. But he could have been talking about the new Legion Memorial Field, home ballpark of the Durand Merchants.

In their first season at the new ball diamond, the Merchants attracted capacity crowds — about 450 fans — to their games on Wednesday, Friday and Sunday nights. Fans parked their cars from behind home plate, skipping around the small and only set of bleachers behind the home team bench, all the way down past the right field pole. The left field lineup was identical, with cars jammed together past the light pole at angles so that fans in the last car could see around the autos down the line to home plate. An eight-foot-high wire fence guarded the baseline from first base to third base and protected some of the cars from foul balls. But past first and third base the cars were naked. Foul balls hit them nearly every game. The streets on each side of the ballpark — East Elm and Dayton — were lined with more parked cars. And for really big games, fans parked their cars on the side lawn of the Larson house across Elm Street.

Earl "Pete" Adleman, the chief umpire of most of the Merchants' games, would park his car in a choice spot at the diamond on a Sunday afternoon so that his wife, Gladys, had a great seat for the game later that night. They lived two blocks from the ballpark and would walk to the car just in time to see batting practice. So would Chet Land and his wife, Creola, and the Mulvain brothers' parents, Lawrence and Mae

Mulvain. As did dozens of others, all vying for the best seats hours before the game began. Many farm families were among the fans. Nearly every Sunday night Edward and Edna Meier drove their daughters Beverly and Delores and son Duane to Legion Field from their farm on Rock Grove Road a couple of miles northwest of town. On Sunday afternoons, George Smith, Jerry Mulvain and one or two others mowed the outfield with hand-pushed mowers. They finally got power mowers a few years later. If there was a heavy rain on game day, George Smith and the Mulvain brothers prepared the field hours before game time. It wasn't unusual for a water puddle to form around home plate. The self-appointed grounds crew tossed gasoline in the puddle and burned off the water.

The biggest pre-game attraction was infield practice. "People came early to watch us," recalled third baseman Wayne Adleman. "We put on a big show. Even the visitors stopped and watched. Sometimes they were in awe as we whipped that ball around the bases. We all could throw, especially Jerry Mulvain. He was a great catcher. We were just a bunch of hometown boys showing off and having fun. Those Rockford teams would come to town thinking they were going to pick up an easy victory over the hick farm boys. Most of the time they went home with their tails between their legs."

It was magic, better than a carnival. Never had so many people gathered for a sporting event in Durand, let alone make so much noise pounding their car horns when the Merchants scored or pitcher Roy Wilke struck out the side. And they were grateful; the collection hat was passed at each game to offset expenses. In a day when a dollar was big money and 50 cents was a large contribution, the collection often totaled $70 plus, more than enough to pay for the $20-an-hour cost of operating the lights.

The Legion's baseball committee lived up to its promise of a concession stand. Lloyd Mulvain discovered an out-building for sale on a Wimpletown farm about 10 miles southeast of Durand. He bought it and had it loaded on a truck and driven to about 25 feet from behind home plate where it was repaired, modified and became the favorite spot of scores of kids. For every foul ball they chased down, they collected a nickel at the concession stand. The fare was minimal: soda, ice cream and popsicles. But who needed more?

Ed Larson lived behind home plate across the street, where fans often gathered to get a drink of water at an outside faucet. So many people used the faucet that water began leaking into the Larson basement.

"So Dad put a hose on the faucet to keep the water away from the house's foundation," Ed recalls.

The Larson yard was pelted by foul balls.

"We would find softballs and baseballs in our flower beds and garden all the time," Ed remembers. "I never did buy a ball when I was growing up."

The team was taking shape and the lineup was looking formidable. It featured Wilke at pitcher, Jerry Mulvain at catcher, Dick Highland at first base, John Hartman at second base, Lloyd Mulvain at shortstop and Wayne Adleman at third base. The outfield consisted of Fred Geiser in left field, Joe Hines in center field, Wayne "Red" Barron or Jack Yaun in right field or even Wilke when he wasn't pitching. Capable reserves who could fill in at many positions included George Smith, his brother Keith "Bud" Smith and Jack McMahon. Highland, Hartman and Hines were related by marriage. Highland married Hartman's sister, Marcia, and Hines married another of Hartman's sisters, Kathleen.

But the Gazette's coverage didn't kick in until late July. A story on May 19 announced a meeting to be held the next week to draw up the schedule for a new softball league that would include the Merchants and teams from Davis, Rock City, Rockton, Pecatonica and Lincoln Park. By the start of the season, Winnebago and Rockford's Hunt & Meyers had replaced Pecatonica and Lincoln Park.

The first game coverage appeared with scores only on June 2 (Durand 20, Farm Bureau 2) and on June 9 under the headline "SOFTBALL SCORES": June 1—Durand 7, Davis 2. June 2—Durand 25, West End Hardware 0. June 7—Bennett Motors (of Rockford) 6, Durand 1. The Gazette gave farmer Leonard Walsh more coverage for being bitten in the left hand by a pig. The eighth grade class that included future Merchant third baseman Kenny Ditzler and Gladys' Bliss' twin sons Fred and Ed got a five-inch story when it received its diplomas. Even young Jim Flynn, age 7, falling while picking cherries and fracturing his left arm, warranted more ink.

Then, on June 23, a two-paragraph account of a no-hitter pitched by Wilke the preceding Sunday took on an entirely different tone from all previous coverage, signaling that a new writer was covering the Merchants:

> "Roy Wilke, Durand's durable right-hander, scaled the heights of pitching perfection Sunday night as Durand shut out (Rockford's) Woodward Governor, 3-0, at the local Legion field.
>
> "Wilke spun a brilliant no-hit, no-run performance, striking out 11 and walking only two. His teammates iced the game for him in the second inning, when they bunched four of their eight hits to score all three of their runs."

No more stories appeared for a month until July 28 when an eight-inch story, the longest account so far, appeared under the two-line, one-column bold headline "Durand Continues Winning Streak." The colorful language reporting on three games continued:

> "The Durand Merchants softball team, rapidly gaining recognition as one of Northern Illinois' best, added three more victories to their string during the past week.
>
> "In a League game July 20 at the Legion field, the scrappy Merchants came through with six runs in the sixth inning to nose out Hunt & Myers, 7-5. (Wayne) Barron and Wilke combined pitching talents and limited the Rockford entry to six hits. Durand collected ten safeties, five of them in the big sixth.
>
> "Sunday night, the locals humbled Maria's, Rockford's 1948 city champs, by a 14-2 count in a non-league game. This game marked the first appearance of the colorful new red and black uniforms, which Durand businesses have donated to the team. A near capacity crowd was on hand to watch the victorious

initiation of the suits.

"Monday night, however, was the big night. In one of the tightest, best-played games ever seen in this area, Durand took a 5-0 decision over Winnebago, after both teams had played nine innings of scoreless ball.

"Roy Wilke again was the shining light for Durand as he weaved his right hand mound magic in shackling Winnebago on five hits. Roy struck out 12, walked only one and was superb in the pinches. Only one man reached third against him. Russ Stringer, Winnebago's able right hander, matched Wilke strike for strike until the roof fell in the tenth.

"(Fred) Geiser started the big inning with a walk; Wilke singled and Jerry Mulvain followed with a line single to drive in the first run of the game. (Dick) Highland smashed a hard liner which the third baseman juggled and the bases were loaded. The second run came in on L. Mulvain's long fly ball and Wayne Adleman then iced the game with a tremendous three-run homer over the left fielder's head.

"The game was replete with fielding gems. Outfielders Barron, (Joe) Hines and (Fred) Geiser all came through with game-saving catches and shortstop Lloyd Mulvain brought the crowd to its feet with a running one-handed catch of a line drive.

"As a result of the past week's games, Durand remains unbeaten and on top of the league. Chuck Tracy has taken over managerial reins of the team and has shown commendable strategy."

The 10-inning game, three more than the standard seven innings, featured the Merchants as the visiting team, giving the last at-bat to the home team Winnebago. This was not unusual; for years Durand played nearly all its games on Legion Field and many times as the visiting team. The week's three victories left the Merchants undefeated in league play for the season but the Gazette didn't report on the number of wins.

The winning streak didn't last long. The Merchants and Wilke dropped two straight games the next week, 4-2 to Rockford Atwood and 5-2 to the Beloit Playdiums. Wilke pitched an outstanding one-hitter against Atwood, allowing only a single. But his seven walks and "slipshod" fielding by his teammates cost Durand the game. Three of Atwood's runs came in the fifth inning when Atwood sandwiched two walks around two errors. Wilke also had two hits, including a double.

In the Beloit game, the Merchants almost became the victim of a no-hitter before the usual overflow crowd at Legion Field. Beloit's pitcher Art Larson hurled five and one-third innings of no-hit, no-run ball before Lloyd Mulvain cracked a triple, scoring his brother Jerry who had gotten on base with an error. Lloyd then scored on a sacrifice fly by Wayne Adleman, giving Durand its only two runs.

Finally, in the Aug. 25 edition of the Gazette, the new writer's identity was revealed in one of the few bylines ever to appear in the paper. The byline read "By Buzz Stauffer." The Merchants were being covered by Charles A. Stauffer, 25, who arrived in Durand in 1947 after working for a print shop in El Paso, Tex. He was born in Susanville, Calif., graduated from high school in South Dakota and enrolled in Pennsylvania State University before enlisting in the Army.

Stauffer saved his first byline for a full-column length story on the biggest game of the year and the biggest in the Merchants' short history. The report appeared at the top of Page One under the first and only two-column headline ever granted the team: "Merchants Upset Rockford's City Champion in 4-3 Thriller Here." The prose flowed:

> "Any and all doubts as to the caliber of ball played by Durand's Merchants were thoroughly and convincingly dispelled here Sunday night when Durand upset Bill's Tavern, Rockford's city champs, in a frenzied, nine-inning 4-3 thriller at Legion Field.
>
> "A jam-packed crowd of cheering, thrilled-crazed fans went home weak and limp from excitement after seeing second baseman Johnny Hartman break up the game with a ninth inning home run blast into right field.
>
> "Durand had tied the game at 3-all in the seventh, after being held to one hit in the first six innings.

"Bud Nielcen, the Tavern's ace twirler and without a doubt the swiftest ever to toe the rubber here, went to the mound in the seventh on the apparently safe side of a 3-0 score and was greeted by a single by L. Mulvain.

"Barron was hit with a pitched ball and Hines worked Nielcen for a free pass to load the bases. Hartman then beat out a high bouncing infield hit and Mulvain came in to score.

"It was a this point that manager Tracy resorted to the shrewd baseball custom of sending a left-handed pinch-hitter against right-handed pitching. Tracy's choice was teen-ager Jack McMahon, who was making his first appearance with the team.

"The youngster fouled off two pitches and then laced a clean hit over third base under the parked cars for a ground rule double, scoring Barron and Hines with the tying runs.

"Bill's Tavern threatened in its half of the ninth when a hit and a misjudged fielder's choice put men on first and third with no outs. Wilke got out of the jam when the next man popped up and the following two grounded out to short.

"Hartman, first man up in Durand's half of the ninth, then laced his game-winning homer and completed the upset of the year.

"The win was determined mainly through two factors: first, the errorless fielding of the locals who handled 25 fielding chances flawlessly; and, second, the control of pitcher Wilke, who walked only four and came through brilliantly in the pinches.

"Special mention, too, should be given Hines and Lloyd Mulvain for their superb play in the field and, of course, Hartman and McMahon."

The game was not just noteworthy for the victory over Rockford's champs. It also marked the first game of Jack McMahon, the youngest player ever to appear in a Merchants' uniform and the only one ever to join the team before graduation from high school. McMahon was 16 years old and had just finished his sophomore year at Durand High

School. He was a superb all-around athlete. And he was fast, faster even than the great center fielder Joe Hines, some people said. Both of them ran as if their hair was on fire. McMahon probably could have beaten Hines in the 60-yard dash to first base but Hines would have won a race to center field.

Stauffer's story also reported on three other Merchant victories that week: a 10-9 win over Rockford's Hunt & Myers with Wilke driving home the winning run with two outs in the bottom of the seventh inning and Dick Highland "collecting a brace of hits," including a two-run homer; a 6-2 victory over Rockford's Williamson Motors when Wilke retired the first 16 batters in a row and finished with 11 strike outs; and a 10-8 win over Rockton with Wilke relieving Barron in the last inning and ending the game by striking out the side.

The week's victories gave the Merchants a 10-0 league record and a 25-6 overall record. It was shaping up to be the greatest season ever.

The latest winning streak reached eight games by the end of August with four more victories. The Merchants crushed the league's second place team, Hunt & Meyers, 16-1 on Wilke's four-hitter. Wilke and Adleman led the offensive attack with three hits apiece. Then it was off to Shannon, about 35 miles southwest of Durand, for a rare road game and a 4-1 victory. Wilke again was in sparkling form, allowing only three hits, with two of them coming in the last inning. Barron led the offense with a two-run homer, "one of the hardest hit balls seen this year," Stauffer wrote.

The third game of the week featured some relief for Wilke, a new "slick windmill pitcher" — Don Nelson—recruited from Rockford. Nelson held the hard-hitting Oakley team to six hits and Highland, Wilke (playing in right field) and McMahon hit home runs as Durand carved out a 15-8 victory. The game was marred by an injury to umpire "Pete" Adleman, who Stauffer wrote "has been doing an efficient job behind the plate all season. Pete was felled by a wild throw in the second inning and suffered a badly bruised nose and cut above the right eye."

The 29th victory of the year, a rare Monday night game, was highlighted by the Merchants' "return to their thrill-a-minute style of play" in their second decision of the year over Russ Stringer and Winnebago, 4-3. Winnebago loaded the bases with one out in the last inning but Wilke, "who has a knack of coming through in the tough spots, got out of the jam on a pop-up and a nice running catch of a fly ball by Jack Yaun." Wilke recorded 10 strikeouts to Stringer's none and with Wayne Adleman led the offense with two hits.

The winning streak continued into September, with three more victories in the month's first week, starting with a close call. The Merchants came from behind twice and scored the winning run in the bottom of the seventh inning on a wild pitch, edging Rockford's all-Negro team, Rapid Auto Laundry, 9-8. Wilke gave up only five hits but was wild, walking nine to go along with 10 strikeouts. He got relief the next night as Nelson won his second straight game and defeated another Rockford Industrial League champion, Ingersoll, 6-2. Stauffer wrote that "Nelson's baffling slow ball, mixed with a windmill speed pitch, had the Ingersoll batters swinging at air most of the evening." But Nelson's career with the Merchants ended as quickly as it started; it was, inexplicably, his last appearance with Durand. Wilke would have to get relief elsewhere. Hartman drove in five of the six runs with a first-inning triple and a fifth-inning three-run home run. Hartman continued his hot hitting — he hit at a .400 pace in his five previous games — with two singles and Highland pitched in with a double and triple as Durand won the third game of the week 12-6 over the Beloit Playdiums, avenging an earlier loss. Wilke held Beloit to five singles. It was Durand's 11th win in a row and the season record now stood at 32 wins and 6 losses.

The Merchants weren't the only big news in 1949. President Truman presented to Congress a domestic program he called the Fair Deal. The Cold War entered its third year following Winston Churchill's declaration at Westminster College in Fulton, Mo., that "an Iron Curtain has descended across Europe." Leo Durocher, manager of the New York Giants, proclaimed that "nice guys finish last" and the Cubs complied again, finishing in last place in the National League. The New York Yankees of Joe DiMaggio defeated Jackie Robinson's Brooklyn Dodgers in the World Series, four games to one in a championship series that ended on Oct. 9, three weeks earlier than today's final playoffs. The Rockford Peaches continued to make history, winning their second league championship with a 75-36 record and their third playoff championship since the All-American Girls Professional Baseball League was begun in 1943.

The Merchants closed out their season before the usual full house at Legion Field on Sept. 25 by playing an East-West All Star Team consisting of players from Rockford, Freeport and Beloit. All Stars or not, they couldn't beat Wilke as Durand won its 13th straight and 34th game of the season, 15-6. It had been a remarkable, record-setting year before huge crowds, making the Merchants the first great athletic team in Durand to draw capacity crowds. They finished with their best overall record, 34 and 6, and won the league championship with a perfect 13 and 0 season. An analysis of the incomplete record — the Gazette covered only 18 of the 40 games but almost all of the ones in August and September — indicated that Wilke most likely won 31 of the 34 games and suffered all six of the losses. Nelson won two games and Barron won at least one. Durand played at least 14 games against 10 Rockford teams and the Beloit Playidums, winning at least 11. Hartman, Adleman, Highland and Wilke himself were the team's best hitters. The Mulvain brothers weren't far behind.

Bill's Barber Shop was buzzing all winter long. How could the Merchants possibly improve on 1949's record? And could Wilke keep pitching a full schedule of games? Didn't the Merchants need to find some relief for him? For those of us who spent as much time chasing foul balls as watching the games, 1950 couldn't come fast enough.

Merchants' team members pose after getting their new uniforms, which were red with black stripes on the pant legs. This photo was taken in 1949 or 1950. Front row, from left, are: left fielder Fred Geiser, catcher Jerry Mulvain, first baseman Dick Highland, right fielder Keith "Bud" Smith, infielder Jack McMahon and shortstop Lloyd Mulvain. Second row: pitcher Roy Wilke, second baseman John Hartman, center fielder Joe Hines, third baseman Wayne Adleman. Back row: outfielder-pitcher Wayne "Red" Barron, right fielder George Smith and right fielder Jack Yaun. (Photo courtesy of Judy Wilke).

Shortstop Lloyd Mulvain's high school graduation picture, taken in 1938. His last name is misspelled.

Second baseman John Hartman's high school graduation picture, taken in 1947.

Right fielder George Smith's high school graduation picture, taken in 1942.

Center fielder Joe Hines' high school graduation picture, taken in 1942.

THE GREATEST SEASON   45

Keith "Bud" Smith, left, and Fred Geiser look over some bowling scores at the Durand bowling alley in the early 1950s. (Photo courtesy of Fred Geiser).

Earl "Pete" Adleman and his wife, Gladys Adleman, on their 50th wedding anniversary, Oct. 10, 1978. Pete was the home plate umpire for most Merchants' games. (Photo courtesy of June Hardesty).

First baseman Dick Highland and his wife, Marcia, on their wedding day, Feb. 23, 1946. (Photo courtesy of Marcia Highland).

DURAND'S MARVELOUS MERCHANTS

COUNTY'S LEADING WEEKLY

Durand Gazette

VOL. LXVI, No. 24 | DURAND, ILLINOIS, THURSDAY, JULY 13, 1950 | WHOLE NO. 2230

Plan Benefit Bakery Sale

Merchants Win 2, Lose To Beloit

County 4-H Show Planned 3 Days

Await Horse Show Saturday

Award Honor Roll Diplomas

Hilltop Opening This Saturday

Church Services

List Committees For Trask Picnic

Softball Calendar

Hartman Market Opening Saturday

4-H Club News

CHAPTER 3

John R. Van Sickle's Durand Gazette

When John R. Van Sickle purchased the Durand Gazette in 1931, its mission had already been established by its previous owner, Charles Bancroft. He published the paper's platform on April 12, 1917:

> "Our Platform: If anyone has — Died, Eloped, Left town, Married, Divorced, Been hurt, Sold a farm, Had a party, Had a baby, Been arrested, Came to town, Bought a home, Entertained company, Formed a partnership, That's NEWS — telephone us at once."

It was a typical news mission for a weekly newspaper and had been since Ben Franklin's era and the Revolutionary War. Even some metropolitan daily newspapers continued to cover minutia long after World War II. The Hartford Courant was famous for being Connecticut's bulletin board even into the 1970s, covering nearly all the state's "chicken dinner" news.

When Bancroft bought the paper in 1907 it was called The Durand Clipper. Before that it was known as the Durand Weekly Clipper (1891), The Durand Record (1890), the Durand Argus (1885), and originally The Durand Patriot (1878). Bancroft changed the paper's name to the Durand Gazette and proclaimed his mission to his readers in the first edition on Thursday, March 28:

> "Just a Few Words: I am here to publish for Durand a newspaper …. The name of the paper is the Durand Gazette and so far as is consistent with earning a reasonable wage for its publisher it will be conducted exclusively in the interests of the town of

Durand and the adjacent territory. In any event, while I control its destinies, it will not be a vehicle for uncalled for criticism, or unjust venting of the spite or malice one individual faction may hold against another. Neither will it be used as a club to convince anyone that I am right and he wrong. With these few explanatory remarks. I respectfully ask the pecuniary support and earnest good will of all those who believe 'the laborer is worthy of his hire.'"

Bancroft also wrote a poem to his readers and published it under the headline "A Welcoming Note:"

"All hail to the Durand Gazette!
Let the town go 'dry' or 'wet.
We need a paper just the same,
And hail thee in the people's name.

We wish to find in thee a friend,
That sticks to right unto the end.
Not trivial, like some old wife's whims,
But ending as well as it begins.

Now, to its patrons I would say,
Just cast your prejudice away,
And take your little pen in hand
To tell what happens round the land.

Just tell the paper what transpires,
From babies' birth to destructive fires.
We have had papers here before,
Indeed, we've had them much galore.

Some sold out while others 'busted,'
But we hope this one may be trusted
To give us all the weekly news
From price of hogs to ladies' shoes;

The price of turnips, beets and onions

With something spicy for the young ones.
And while we're with the little folks,
Don't hold too tight upon their jokes.

Don't try to keep their noises under,
They will yell in spite of thunder.
And here crops out that other truth;
Men are but boys of older youth.

So let the town go 'dry' or 'wet,'
We'll shout, All hail Durand's Gazette!
And here my rhyming's done, par se,
And sign me simply just B.B."

Van Sickle never intended to become a weekly newspaper owner. He grew up in Durand, graduated from Durand High School and attended the School of Journalism at the University of Illinois in Champaign-Urbana, graduating in 1931. He worked two summers at the Rockford Daily Republic and hoped for a full-time position after graduation. But by then the Rockford daily newspapers had merged, the Depression was well underway and there were no jobs available anywhere.

Bancroft was more than 70 years old and ready to retire. He had sold the paper to his son but was forced to return from California to reclaim it when his son failed to make any payments. Still wanting out of the business, he approached Van Sickle in June 1931 and tried to convince him of the advantages of owning his own business. Van Sickle balked. He explained his reluctance in a three-page introduction to a book of his favorite columns published in 1980, six years after he retired:

> "I was not interested. I had studied reporting and editorial writing in school but had not stressed the business side of newspaper publishing. Oh, I had had simple basic courses in advertising and newspaper business practices, but I really did not care to go into business when I knew so little about the publishing field. Furthermore, I did not have any money to invest in a newspaper.
>
> "That summer I had two jobs for awhile, helping paint and put

on a new roof on my step-grandmother's home in Durand. By Sept. 1, I had the magnificent capital of $66.93 accumulated and still owed some $900 on my college education.

"Winter was coming on. Wishing to return to California and knowing that I had not found a job, Mr. Bancroft approached me again about purchasing the business. He dropped the asking price from $5,000 to $4,500 and offered to sell with a $500 down payment with monthly payments of $50 which would include interest on the unpaid balance at six percent.

"Desperate to find something to do, I decided to take the plunge. Because my step-grandmother owned property and would sign a note with me I was able to borrow $600. I paid Bancroft $500 and started in business, then, with $166.93 capital. How foolish can a young man be?"

Thus a U of I journalism graduate who intended to become a reporter and who knew next to nothing about running any business, not even a newspaper, became a young press lord and published his first issue on Oct. 8, 1931.

Fortunately, he got lucky. But as former Texas football coach Darrell Royal said, "You've got to be in position for luck to happen. Luck doesn't go around looking for a stumblebum." And Van Sickle was no stumblebum. He had purchased a weekly newspaper — actually two because The Davis Leader was published at the Durand plant — that had been lax in keeping up the subscription lists and many subscribers were in arrears. He also benefited from the recent "new look" of the paper; it now had headlines on news stories that eliminated hard-to-read columns of unrelated items. The heads had to be set by hand. But he got lucky again — he had taken one course at Illinois on printing and learned what was called the California job case. By printing only headlines on Page One, he could do it himself. Headlines on inside pages would have required more employees, which he couldn't afford. Furthermore, unlike his competition, The Pecatonica News, the Gazette had a linotype machine that cast the lines of news type. The owners of the News were setting the entire paper by hand, letter by letter, at a much slower pace. The Gazette's new, modern look combined with a campaign to entice subscribers to pay past bills generated badly needed new revenue even though it was but $1 a year per subscription. For three days in July 1932, the Gazette held a special sale. Subscribers could pay for the paper with eggs. Five dozen would purchase a six-month subscription and 10 dozen would buy a year's subscription.

But the biggest break that Van Sickle got was that he took over operation of the Gazette during the Depression, the worst economic downturn in the history of the country. What was a horrible time for farmers turned out to be a fortunate one for weekly newspapers. Farmers were going broke and insurance companies were foreclosing on farms every week. By law, the insurance firms were required to publish legal notices in advance of an auction. Most chose to publish every week in the weekly papers because their advertising rates were much less expensive than those of daily papers. That revenue kept many weekly newspapers afloat in the 1930s.

It wasn't long before the Gazette became a family affair:

> "Soon, my mother was calling people on the phone for news items and my dad came in to help mail the papers on Wednesday afternoon and night.
>
> "As the business volume grew both of my parents became more active in the business. Mother became the bookkeeper and Dad became the all-around man who could do, and did, almost everything around the plant. He kept the machinery going. In later years his chief responsibility was as proofreader. He could not be beaten at that. In fact he read his last proof for the papers when he was 87 years old."

Keeping the machinery going could be a full-time job on some days for Van Sickle's father. Accidents were all too common:

> "Until the newspaper went offset, hand-fed presses were used. That meant a lot of monotonous work. The first such press did not have a throw-off lever. When you missed getting in a sheet of paper, you had to stop the press and wipe the ink off the plate before resuming the presswork.

"Only two pages could be printed at one time. The purchase of a four-page press was a big step forward and it had a throw-off lever as well. I recall that we had to tear down a portion of a brick wall in order to get the new press in our building.

"The page forms (containing the type) had to be locked into place on the bed of the press. One day, just as I was about to lock up the pages I was called to the phone. Thoughtlessly, I rushed up to the front office and Dad, thinking that I had completed my job, stepped up to the press and pushed the button to take a page proof.

"Crash — the outside pages slid off with the first motion of the press. I came running back to the press. What a sight. The metal forms hung in space with type dropping out of them.

"The accident stripped the teeth on a drive gear of the press. Not only did we have to make a trip to Chicago to replace the gear but a considerable amount of type had to be reset. Even though the papers were a day late that week, the accident could have had even more disastrous results had some of the press been broken that could not have been replaced.

"Another type of accident occurred occasionally when someone would accidentally leave a makeup rule or coin key on top of the type on the bed of the press. As soon as the press was started there would be a thud and some smashed type."

Over the years Van Sickle expanded the business, joining the manager of three Ogle County weekly newspapers at Stillman Valley, Byron and Leaf River in jointly selling advertising at a group rate. Later, long after the Merchants were past their heyday, he formed Van Sickle's Associated Publishers, Inc., and added weeklies in German Valley, Orangeville, Winslow, Kirkland, Winnebago and Rockton.

In the early years, the Gazette printed what was known as readyprints — two or four syndicated pages furnished by the Western Newspaper Union that featured general world news and features. But

Van Sickle dropped them a few years later; his weeklies were producing enough local news and advertising to fill all the pages.

And, as Bancroft had stated in 1917, the Gazette was interested in printing items big and small — nothing was too trivial. Take, for instance, one of the most unusual news items ever published by any newspaper, this one on June 29, 1950, under the one-column headline "TRAFFIC COUNT IS HEAVY":

> "Mrs. Tobe Tallakson noticed the traffic was heavy by her home Sunday afternoon, so she started to count the vehicles as they passed, going both in and out of town. In about two hours she had counted 896."

A story in the next column warranted a three-line, one-column headline:

> "HUNDREDS VISIT SCOTT FARM
> TO VIEW HOLE
> IN THE EARTH"
>
> "Since Aubrey Scott, who lives on Owen Center Road, discovered a strange hole in the earth on his farm, hundreds of people have visited the farm.
>
> "Mr. Scott discovered the hole while cultivating corn. The depth of the opening has not been determined by those investigating it. Apparently, there is some sort of an underground cavern there."

More common was the news of who was entertaining whom, who visited hospital patients, who was injured in accidents, all the births and deaths and the activity at Scout meetings, 4-H meetings, county fairs, horse shows, rodeos, band concerts, churches and schools. Sometimes it was simply the reporting of a good deed, common in rural America in a much simpler time, such as the one that occurred July 11, 1950:

> "Ten neighbors of Mr. and Mrs. Raymond Clark, their wives and children, totaling 38, gathered at the Clark home Tuesday afternoon, July 11, and put up 25 acres of hay.
>
> "The families brought with them three balers, six tractors and

five wagons.

> "The Clark family have (sic) not been ill or suffered any misfortune, but the neighbors had their haying done and he didn't."

Much of the Gazette's news read like the writings of the Duke of Paducah, a humorist who in real life was Durand's own Guy Walker. From 1946 to 1959, the Duke wrote 1,883 news items called "Durand Doings" at the tail end of the Chicago Tribune's "Wake of the News" column. That column was written by the legendary Tribune sports editor Arch Ward and then later by David Condon.

"Durand Doings" often used real names and places but contained fictitious events. Some readers thought "Durand Doings" was a boring recital of small-town trivia. Others weren't sure if the Duke was poking fun at small-town life or celebrating it. Mostly, he was doing both.

The Duke described Durand as the second best place in the world to be born. The only better place, he said, would have been Louisville's Churchill Downs, about which he proclaimed "you ain't never been nowhere and you ain't never seen nothing 'till you been to the Kentucky Derby."

Unlike "Durand Doings," the Gazette focused on facts and real events, many much more interesting than fiction. Take, for instance, this one published on May 19, 1949:

> "Leonard Walsh was bitten on his left hand by a pig Saturday morning. Blood poisoning set in at once and he was taken to St. Francis hospital, Freeport, that afternoon. With the use of modern drugs, Mr. Walsh is making a satisfactory and speedy recovery and was able to come home Tuesday."

Or this one, published about my dad on Sept. 29, 1949:

> "Following the first week of bowling with an electric-eye foul indicator, Durand keglers appeared unanimous in their approval of the device. It may have been that bowlers used an extra ounce of caution, but fouls were few and far between during the past week.

"Ward Waller, the Palmyra Pistol, claimed the honor of being the first to 'buzz' the eye, when he gave it a test, following its installation here.

"Cracked Waller, 'I was right on the beam.'"

The Duke of Paducah couldn't make up stuff that good.

Much of the news was placed item after item under a headline simply naming the town from which it was filed. Mostly that news was printed on the inside pages but sometimes it was published on Page One. The Gazette covered several area towns, including Davis, Rock City, Ridott, Shirland and Winnebago. The amount of news was related more to who was the correspondent than to events of the week. If a town was lucky to have a prolific correspondent it got extensive coverage. A lax correspondent meant far less news.

Van Sickle finally got full use of his journalism degree 10 years after buying the Gazette when he wrote his first weekly editorial column on Aug. 28, 1941. He called it "In This Column," by John R. Van Sickle and placed it at the top of Page One in the first column. A logo depicting a typewriter and containing his byline rested atop each column he wrote.

Van Sickle's column revealed just how different he was from a typical weekly editor of the era. It wasn't just that he was a sophisticated and erudite editor in rural America. He had a passion for national politics, American public policy, global issues before that became fashionable decades later to care about, U.S. public policy, morals and religion, especially the Methodist variety. He was a Methodist lay leader and delegate to state and national conferences for years. He wrote about his vacations, speeches by anyone who struck his fancy or books that he had read. Unlike most weekly editors, he rarely wrote about his town or any public policy issues confronting it. In his collection of his favorite columns published in 1980, six years after he retired, not once does the name Durand appear in any one of them. He could have written any of those columns from nearly anywhere in America.

Perhaps that's why many Durand folks thought of Van Sickle as somewhat aloof, even a bit snobbish. It didn't help that he moved to Rockford in 1948 so that his children could attend what he thought were better schools than those in Durand. Or that he was engaged in civic activity, but mostly in Rockford. A small-town editor commuting from a big city would not enamor him to many of his readers.

And while writing a column is hard work — the great sports columnist Red Smith compared it to squeezing blood out of a vein a drop at a time — he would occasionally lapse into taking the easy way out in his columns. The most outrageous example began on June 9, 1949:

> "Illinois' first press and radio field day was held at Champaign-Urbana, Friday afternoon and Saturday morning, June 3 and 4, with the College of Agriculture at the University of Illinois, Farm and Home Advisers of the state, and the Extension Service in Agriculture and Home Economics as hosts.
>
> "Your writer was the guest of the Stephenson and Winnebago County Farm Bureaus and was conducted on tour by V. J. Banter, Stephenson County's farm adviser. Art Hanstrom of radio station WFRL at Freeport complete the trio that rode to Champaign in Mr. Banter's car.
>
> "The exterior of my balding head was treated generously to a coat of sun burn and tan. The interior was crammed with thousands of ideas, some of which I shall endeavor to pass along to my readers.
>
> "I shall not attempt to tell all in a single week, but the ground that I fail to cover this week will be gone over in future columns."

Little did readers realize that the "future columns" on Van Sickle's visit to the university would continue for six straight weeks. He expounded on such topics as how to write good farm stories; the latest in airplane spraying and weed, fly, household pest and corn borer control; how to choose the best eggs; nutrition experiments with rats; how farmers could reduce cattle-feed risks with such advice as "avoid buying stale cattle;" a detailed description of how a cow digests hay — it went on and on and on until July 21 for about a total of 120 column inches. Some of the topics would have appealed to his farmer readers, to be sure, but it's difficult to imagine anyone was interested in six straight weeks of show-and-tell at the university agricultural extension.

In truth, Van Sickle found readers' interests hard to gauge. After writing a column for 10 years, he lamented on Aug. 23, 1951, the lack of response his column generated:

> "Goodness knows, I write this column week in and week out without hearing anything about it. I often wonder if anyone ever reads it. As one writer said the other day, writing is ninetenths hard work and one-tenth inspiration. It is difficult to fill this corner of the paper each week. I know the result seldom indicates the perspiration that has gone into its concoction."

Fortunately, a lightning bolt in the form of a satisfied reader struck him:

> "I was attending one of the recent outdoor concerts of the Rockford Symphony orchestra at Sinnissippi Park. I ran across one of my Ogle County readers.
>
> "She said — Mr. Van Sickle, I want to tell you how much I enjoy reading your column each week —
>
> "That was the ethereal moment. That was the moment that repaid me for the hours of struggling with my typewriter to get it to write down something that my subscribers would read, and that would be worthwhile. That was a moment in a lifetime."

The Ogle County reader wasn't his only satisfied customer. My parents read Van Sickle's column and the Gazette faithfully. They were interested in many of the same issues. They also read three daily newspapers: The Rockford Morning Star, The Freeport Journal-Standard and The Beloit Daily News. My mother, Esther Waller, was a correspondent for the Journal-Standard and the Daily News for about 15 years. My dad, Ward Waller, was a rural mail carrier for 29 years and an officer in the state association in charge of the group's insurance programs. He also subscribed to the Congressional Record to keep informed of the latest issues in Congress.

Sometimes one of Van Sickle's sons filled in as a guest columnist.

In July of 1952 Van Sickle had to attend a church conference so he had his son, John B. Van Sickle, listen to the Republican Convention on the radio and take notes. John B. took 54 pages of notes and his father simply published his running summary as a column. A year later Van Sickle was gone for three weeks and John B. wrote three consecutive columns on his experiences attending Boys' State, a weeklong assembly of young men and women learning the intricacies of government and democracy.

When it came to politics, Van Sickle could be insightful. He predicted that Gen. Dwight Eisenhower would defeat Ohio Sen. Robert Taft for the Republican nomination for president in 1952. But he erroneously thought that Gov. Adlai Stevenson of Illinois would accept the Democratic nomination only if Taft defeated Eisenhower. Van Sickle often quoted at length other writers' opinions on elections and politics, downplaying his own opinions that seemed as knowledgeable as the experts he quoted.

One of the best column's Van Sickle ever wrote was on July 12, 1956, a day before the beginning of the Durand Centennial Celebration. It was about Durand:

> "Villages have problems peculiar to them, yet universal in that so many villages have the same problems. Because this is the week that Durand is observing its Centennial and because the historical information has been covered in official Centennial booklet, your writer is concerned here with the problems that Durand faces as its second century begins.
>
> "Most residents would agree with me that these are the major problems that need to be solved:
>
> "Need for a modern sewer system.
>
> "Need for a medical clinic that will attract a resident physician.
>
> "Need for more school space as the high school enrollment grows in the near future.
>
> "Need for a bank.

He noted plans for a bank were well underway and that the town's drug store had closed and the only doctor had moved away. He also reported on the difficulty of building a sewer system. He wound up his column with a rallying cry:

> "You may have seen the signs that read: We can do anything that is possible right away; the impossible takes us a little longer. This is about it. The impossible problem of building a sewer system will take us a little longer.
>
> "Durand has demonstrated its wholehearted cooperation in preparing for the Centennial that its citizens can accomplish much, can make sacrifices to get a job well done.
>
> "While much of the time during Centennial observance is spend looking backward, I would like to look ahead and see the area's residents accomplishing the impossible. It can be done."

Within two years all but the sewer system had been achieved. Durand State Bank opened on Feb. 1, 1957. Its officers were Ted Haggerty, president; Mrs. Floy B. Chapin, vice president; William W. Smith, cashier; and Mrs. Jan Shirk, assistant. Joining Haggerty, Mrs. Chapin and Smith on the board were Robert Dobler, Donald Flynn, Ellis Greene and Algot Larson. In 1958, a new medical center with its founding physician, Dr. Richard Harvey, opened next to the bank. By the end of the year a new wing had been added to the elementary school to create a new high school.

Completing the sewer system took much longer. The four-phase project was started in March of 1976 at a cost of $259,000. The total project would cost $830,000, the equivalent of $3.6 million today.

Had Van Sickle written more often on the challenges facing Durand he would have wielded more influence in solving its problems and added readers to his column. But it wasn't clear he really wanted more readers.

In a column on Aug. 9, 1951, he wrote about the evils of college sports and criticized newspapers for over-emphasizing sports in attempt to get more readers:

"Sports pages and sport sections have grown in metropolitan papers along with the growing emphasis on sports everywhere. Publishers have stressed sports because more and more people were interested, and that meant selling more papers, more reader interest.

"All this stress on 'big' games has led to nationwide betting pools and gambling. Now comes the expulsion of 90 United States military cadets at West Point for cribbing in examinations. One spokesman has declared that the football team was the cause of the violation of the honor system. The members of the football squad just could not keep up with the pressure to produce a winning football team and keep up with their strenuous schedule of studies at the same time.

"It seems that with this additional evidence that we might be convinced that it was about time that our county de-emphasized its sports programs.

"Why do we play games in the first place? Do we play to win or do we play for the fun of it? We have been playing to win! And this is where we have been putting the emphasis in the wrong place.

"We need to teach our children to play games for the joy of playing, not for the thrill of winning. We cannot always be winners. We must learn to lose as well.

"This philosophy applies to more aspects of life than sports. We cannot all be presidents, we cannot always be 'sitting on top of the world.' We must learn to work and play for the satisfaction there is in doing the best that we can. We will not be criticized if we have done our best, even if it has not brought us success."

Van Sickle obviously did not appreciate the values learned by participating in sports or realize that a great athletic team such as the Merchants could inspire an entire town. His philosophy about sports would put him at odds with reporter Buzz Stauffer and eventually threaten the coverage of the Merchants in the next few years.

CHAPTER 4

Running Out of Adjectives

A capacity crowd jammed Legion Field on May 14 for the opening game of the 1950 season, anticipating a continuation of last year's winning streak. But, alas, it was not to be.

Despite outhitting the Freeport Eagles 12 to 4, the Merchants suffered a 13-8 loss. Roy Wilke, coming off a 31-6 season, had everything except control. He pitched five innings of no-hit ball and struck out 11. But he also walked 11. Outfielder Bernie Figi, playing his first season for the Merchants, relieved Wilke in the sixth inning with the score tied 6-6. But Figi gave up four hits and a pair of walks. That combined with five errors gave Freeport its deciding margin. As usual, reporter Buzz Stauffer never mentioned who made the errors. Perhaps it was a reflection of the former Gazette owner's philosophy of "not being a vehicle for uncalled criticism."

Third baseman Wayne Adleman started off the season with a hot bat, hitting a home run, triple and a single. Left fielder Fred Geiser, center fielder Joe Hines and shortstop Lloyd Mulvain each collected two hits.

The big blow to the Merchants, however, was the injury suffered by catcher Jerry Mulvain, who stopped a foul tip on the thumb of his catching hand. X-rays after the game showed he had suffered a badly bruised bone and would be out of action for an indefinite time.

Mulvain was an outstanding ballplayer and a terrific catcher, the epitome of what the greatest shortstop in major league history, Honus Wagner, said in 1908 of being a ballplayer: "There ain't much to being a ballplayer if you're a ballplayer." Mulvain played baseball, usually shortstop, for Pecatonica as well as softball for the Merchants. During a typical week, he played three nights for the Merchants and four or five baseball games including doubleheaders. He frequently played a Sunday afternoon baseball game and then caught for the Merchants Sunday night. He carried a uniform in his car at all times so he would not have to return home to change for the next game. Mulvain had a cannon for an arm; he threw better than any catcher in the region. He and his brother Lloyd, when he played third, picked off a lot of runners. "We had a signal," Jerry said, "We'd catch them off guard." He also caught plenty of runners off guard at first base.

Lloyd also played baseball and for a few years was the catcher for the Shirland team in the Andy Gump League, named after a cartoon character. Jerry thought Lloyd was good enough to make it to the major leagues despite his small stature — he was about 5 foot 6 inches tall. But Lloyd already had a family and had given up on any idea of playing professional baseball. Jerry played softball from 1946 when he was discharged from the Marines until age 46 in 1972, the last five years for Winnebago. "Playing ball was my life," Mulvain said. "That's what I lived for. I don't know why my wife put up with it."

Losing their star catcher didn't slow down the Merchants. High school coach and assistant principal Don Hubbartt filled in as catcher the next week and had two hits as Durand defeated Rockford Palm Garden 13-8. Adleman's bat continued to smoke; he had three hits including two home runs. Wilke and newcomer Bill Huddleston, a business teacher at Durand High School, shared pitching duties. The following Sunday Mulvain returned to the lineup and the Merchants beat one of the best Rockford teams, Ingersoll, 8-5. Mulvain contributed a home run, as did his brother Lloyd and Adleman, his fourth home run in the last three games. But the big blow came from first baseman Dick Highland, whose three-run home run in the fifth inning broke up a 5-5 tie. Huddleston pitched a complete game, scattering nine hits and striking out 10. It looked as if the Merchants had found some relief for Wilke.

The following week the Merchants reeled off three more victories, running their winning streak to five. Wilke preserved a 5-3 win over Illinois Sporting Goods of Freeport by striking out the Freeport right fielder with the bases loaded in the seventh inning. In all, Wilke rang up 15 strikeouts and gave up only five hits. Figi led the hitters with a triple and a single and Jerry Mulvain and Adleman each had a hit.

The big game of the week came on Friday, May 26, and Stauffer described the tension:

> "In one of the finest games ever played on the local diamond, the Merchants edged Smith Oil of Rockford, 1-0, as Bill Huddleston, the sensational new 'find' of the locals, stopped the Oilers on four hits.
>
> "A Friday night crowd, of the usual capacity variety, saw Wayne Adleman slam a towering home run into left field (there were no outfield fences) for the only tally in a great mound duel between Huddleston and the Smith's Schuldt.
>
> "Joe Hines, who roams center field like an antelope, also shared in the evening's heroics with a running catch of what looked to be a home run drive by the Smith Oil third baseman, Conger, in the sixth inning with another Oiler on second. Hines had previously made a pair of great attempts on shoestring catches to add thrills to an already thrill-packed game.
>
> "Huddleston, local high school teacher from Macomb, Ill., struck out 13 in the course of the evening and twice pitched his way out of holes after the lead-off batter had reached second with no outs in the third and sixth innings. His control was letter perfect; he did not give up a walk and his acrobatic fast ball had the Oilers baffled. "Adleman collected two of the five hits gathered off Schuldt while (Johnny) Hartman, (Jack) Yuan and Huddleston got the other three, all singles."

The Merchants finished the week with a 5-1 record when they massacred Rock City 19-4 with Wilke allowing only three hits and striking out eight. The hitting stars included Adleman, Hartman and Hines with three hits each, including a home run by Hines, and Dick

Highland and Wilke, with a home run apiece.

Then, for some unknown reason, the coverage of the Merchants disappeared for three weeks. Perhaps Stauffer was on vacation. Whatever the reason, no stories about the Merchants appeared until June 22, when it became apparent Durand had lost two of the three intervening games.

The Gazette was filled with other news, including this one paragraph story about Wilke's first cousin under the headline "Around the Town":

> "Clair Wilke killed three badgers on his farm southwest of Durand last Saturday."

It also reported on an initiation ceremony being planned by Boy Scout Troop 29 at the Laona Forest Preserve. The Scouts were to assemble in town and hike out to the preserve, about three miles northwest of Durand. Boys to be initiated as Tenderfoot Scouts included Fredrick Meier, Norman Chilton, Danny Waller, Jack Walsh, Bob Haggerty, Donnie Waller, Kenny Waller, and the Peterson twins, Trude and Trudane.

The Merchants also made news with the unexplained departure of their new-found pitcher Huddleston. It's likely he simply left the area after the schools closed for the summer. So the Merchants returned to their one-man pitching corps, Wilke, and won two straight games during the week of June 11. Highland's seventh-inning, two-out single drove in Fred Geiser with the winning run in a thrilling 5-4 victory over Rockford's Central Illinois Electric & Gas. Wilke hooked up in a pitching duel with Bud Nielcen, who had pitched Bill's Tavern to the Rockford city championship a year earlier. Each allowed only five hits, with Nielcen leading in strikeouts, 8-4. But Wilke proved toughest in the clutch. He also tied the game at 4-4 with a home run in the fifth inning.

Wilke saved his best for Sunday night when he pitched the third no-hit game of his career and defeated Rockford's Free Sewing Machine 8-0. He faced only 24 batters in the seven-inning shutout, retiring the first 12 men in order, and struck out 10. Adleman once again led the offense with a two-run home run.

So how good was Wilke?

"Pretty damn good," said Adleman. "He was a great competitor and had the confidence of all the players."

Wilke's style was unique; he called it "the wheel" and always pitched without wearing a glove. His right bicep — on his pitching arm—was twice as big as his left. My brother, Steve Waller, became a student of softball pitching when his daughters Julie and Elizabeth became fast-pitch softball pitchers in the 1980s. He described the two most common pitching styles and "the wheel" this way:

> "Most softball pitchers used the windmill style, in which the ball is brought in a total circle around the pitcher's head. The idea is to generate arm speed and thus propel the ball at a greater speed. In the sling shot style, the ball is brought back from the body of the pitcher to a vertical position over the head. It is then 'slung' back underarm toward home plate.
>
> "With 'the wheel,' the ball starts in the pitcher's hands in front of his body. From there the pitcher rotates the arms in a horizontal circle as a hoop around his hips. The arms go from the front of the body to the back. Then they return to the front as a wheel rotating in a horizontal plane. The first key to the pitch is hiding the ball from the batter. At no time during delivery is the ball in sight. A second key is the rotation of the shoulders and the hips. The final key is that when the ball is delivered the hips and shoulders are pointed toward third base (for a right-handed pitcher). When the ball passes the front of the body there is no resistance. This allows for the most important part of the pitch, the wrist snap. Roy was fast but his effectiveness was the movement he created on the ball as it approached the plate. This came from different grips and different wrist snaps."

Like all great softball pitchers, Wilke didn't just deliver the ball. He commanded, controlled and dominated hitters. That's what distinguished fast-pitch softball from other team sports. No other game had a position so dominant as the pitcher in softball. Wilke's pitches were fairly fast — 55 to 65 miles an hour from the 46 feet to home plate, compared with a good baseball pitcher's fastball from of 95 miles an hour from 60 feet six inches. Yet many softball pitchers were faster than

Wilke, 70 miles an hour or more. But only a few could make the ball "dance" like Wilke.

He released the ball just barely off the ground and it rose all the way to the plate. When a hitter first saw the pitch, it looked as if it would be about belt high in the strike zone. But by the time it got to the plate it was shoulder high or higher and left the hitter swinging at air.

Wilke had come by this pitching style naturally in the third grade. He set up batters with various pitches, lured them like fish with bait, and then, in one final pitch, demoralized them. Moreover, Wilke had excellent control. Said Jerry Mulvain, "As a catcher, you just sat there and didn't move to catch his ball. Unlike 'Red' Barron, (nicknamed for his fiery red hair and temper) who was all over the place, wild. I was exhausted catching him, up and down with each pitch. And it got worse when he lost his temper, which was quite often."

Left fielder Fred Geiser summed it up: "Without Wilke and Jerry Mulvain, we were just another team." As a witness to scores of games and a ballplayer myself, I would rephrase that: Without Wilke, the Mulvain brothers and Wayne Adleman, the Merchants were just another good team.

Among the several pitchers in the region throwing even faster than Wilke were Vernon "Bullet" Kirk of several Freeport teams, Bud Nielcen of Rockford's Bill's Tavern, Ralph "Rosie" Rosenke of Rockford's Greenlee Brothers and Roscoe teams, Charlie Long of the Rockford's Parker Sporting Goods, Art Larson of the Beloit Playidums, Bennie Renaldo who pitched for a couple of Rockford teams, one-armed Vern Simmer of Davis and Irish Grove, Deacon Davis, the great basketball player who pitched for the Freeport Eagles, and Wilke's teammate, Bill Huddleston, who was an excellent hurler but lacked the ball movement that Wilke featured.

Only Kirk, and possibly Long, was better than Wilke. Kirk was phenomenal. He was recruited by Freeport's Henney Hearse Co. in 1949 from Charleston, W. Va. He pitched several no-hitters and in 1950, hurling for the Freeport Merchants, struck out the first 15 batters and a total of 25 of 28 in a 9-inning one-hitter and defeated the Milwaukee Pabst Brewers, 7-0.

As good as Kirk and Wilke were, they were no match for the two greatest softball pitchers I ever witnessed — Eddie Feigner of The King and His Court and Harvey Sterkel of the Aurora Sealmasters. Feigner and his four-man team fielding a catcher, pitcher, first baseman and shortstop barnstormed around the world for 61 years starting in 1946, playing against conventional nine-man teams. He won more than 10,000 games, pitched 930 no-hitters and 238 perfect games and struck out 141,517 batters pitching from the pitcher's mound, second base, center field, behind his back, between his legs and blindfolded. His fastball once was clocked at 104 miles an hour. You had to see it to believe it. Even then you weren't sure it was real.

Sterkel led the Sealmasters to four American Softball Association national fast-pitch championships from 1956 to 1969, during which time he won 345 games and lost only 33. He struck out 5,212 in 2,599 innings, pitched 60 no-hitters and 15 perfect games and compiled a 0.34 earned run average.

With Huddleston's departure, Wilke was back in action full-time the third week in June, racking up three straight victories against three tough teams. First he beat Podunk College of Rockford, 3-2, limiting the Podunkers to five hits and striking out nine. Second baseman Johnny Hartman drove in two of the runs and scored the third with a triple and a double. The only other hits were Jerry Mulvain's triple and Figi's single. Next Wilke shut out Rockford's National Lock 4-0 on a three-hitter. He faced only 26 hitters in the seven-inning game, allowed only one hitter to reach second base and forced 14 batters to pop-up his fastball. Barron, playing left field, was the hitting star, driving in three of Durand's runs with a home run and a single. Wilke finished the week by leaving reporter Stauffer searching for words:

> "In one of the great mound duels ever witnessed at the local field, Roy Wilke edged Freeport's spectacular Negro star, Deacon Davis, as the Merchants topped the Freeport Eagles 3-2 in nine innings Sunday.
>
> "A tremendous crowd alternately held their breath and roared their lungs out as the two great mound stars slanted even-stephen

ball for eight full innings.

"An unearned run in the last of the ninth, coming as a result of a pair of bobbles by Freeport's third sacker, spelled the difference in the tense battle.

"Wilke, who is rapidly surpassing this reporter's vocabulary of adjectives, stopped the Eagles on eight hits and, in so doing, ended the unbeaten record of the Freeport entry, which had won eight straight, including an early season win over the locals. Roy set 16 men down on strikes and won his own game with a line drive single, scoring (Joe) Hines from third. Hines had led off the ninth by reaching first on an error and had advanced to third when the Eagles' third baseman bobbled (Fred) Geiser's ground ball.

"The Merchants again played errorless ball in the field and came up with an all-important double play in the eighth. After Winters had opened Freeport's eighth with a single, Wilke whiffed the next batter but was then worked for a walk, putting men on first and second with one out. H. Winters then stroked what looked to be a perfect Texas League hit behind short only to have Barron grab it on the dead run and double the runner off second to retire the side.

"Wayne Adleman returned to his long ball driving by pounding out a pair of triples while Joe Hines rapped a double and a single and Lloyd Mulvain chipped in with a pair of one-baggers."

The three victories gave the Merchants six straight wins and a 12-3 record for the season.

The Merchants made it seven wins in a row by defeating Donor's Garage of Beloit 5-1 on Wednesday, June 28, as Wilke pitched a four-hitter and struck out nine. The game was closer than the score. It was tied 1-1 in the sixth inning when Durand scored four runs, three of them coming on a bases-loaded double by George "Chesty" Smith. Lloyd Mulvain and Smith each had two hits.

And then the Merchants ran into a tornado in the form of ace pitcher Charley Long, who lived up to his advance billing as one of the region's best pitchers. Long held Durand to one hit — Adleman's double in the fourth inning — and shut out the Merchants 8-0. It didn't help that Wilke, with a sore back muscle, and first baseman Dick Highland were absent. Figi pitched credible ball for the Merchants but was hampered by five Durand errors.

But the Merchants bounced back on Sunday, July 2, "...before a jam-packed crowd, estimated as the largest ever to witness at game at Legion Field," as Wilke hurled a four-hitter in defeating Illinois Sporting Goods of Freeport 4-2. Durand managed only four singles but was aided by five Freeport errors in running its season record to 14-4.

If Charlie Long was a tornado, Art Larson was a severe thunderstorm. Larson faced only 24 Durand batters in seven innings as the Beloit Playdiums defeated the Merchants 2-1 on Wednesday, July 5. Wilke gave up no earned runs and only three hits to Larson's four but suffered his first loss of the season in nine games. Durand rebounded 15-14 against Rockford's Woodward Governor on Friday, July 7, in a sloppy game marked by 13 errors, eight by the Merchants. Figi pitched for the Merchants but was chased in the second inning when Woodward Governor scored 10 runs. Barron, pitching for the first time all year, took over with one out and pitched top-flight ball the rest of the game. Adleman, Hines, Lloyd Mulvain and Hartman each had two hits. Wilke returned on Sunday, July 9, struck out 13 and gave up only four hits as The Merchants crushed Rockford's Palm Gardens, 12-4. Lloyd Mulvain had three hits and Hines slammed a home run and a triple. Stauffer wound up his story with a salute to some volunteers:

> "Pete Adleman, Tip Tracy, Bump Sarver and Rollie Mulvain continue their commendable work as umpires, while another thankless job, that of official scorer, has been capably handled by Abe Mulvain, Carl Nuss and Bump Sarver."

Virgil "Abe" Mulvain attended some Merchant games but Stauffer most likely was wrong about Abe being an official score keeper, according to his brother, Jerry Mulvain.

Barron repeated his performance the next week in his first start of the season. He pitched a two-hitter and struck out the side in the seventh inning as the Merchants defeated Rockford's Smith Oil for the second time this season, 2-1. Hines provided the winning run with a towering home run to left field in the fourth inning. Adleman and Lloyd Mulvain had Durand's only other hits.

Hines was a remarkable center fielder. He not only was fast — he and Jerry Mulvain were the team's best base stealers — but was catlike quick and an acrobat in making shoestring catches. It was almost impossible to get a ball past him. He had a terrific arm and was by far the Merchants' best outfielder, though Fred Geiser was as steady in left field as Hines was spectacular in center. The two of them were outfield fixtures for several years.

Hines also was a very good hitter, one of the team's best. And he was strong, especially for a small, wiry person — he was about 5 feet 8 inches tall and couldn't have weighed more than 150 pounds. I remember several visits to his farm four miles north of Durand on State Line Road with my parents and brothers to buy eggs. The driveway to the farm was severely uphill and at the top of it rested a cement water tank that frequently held large cans of fresh milk being cooled awaiting to be picked up by a dairy. A full can weighed at least 80 pounds and Hines was dazzling as he repeatedly lifted one in each arm out of the tank and into the milk truck.

Barron continued to pitch well in Wilke's absence, probably caused by a sore arm. On Friday, July 21, "Big Red" pitched a one-hitter and struck out eight as the Merchants lashed out 13 hits and crushed Freeport Lincoln-Mercury 17-2. Lloyd Mulvain led Durand's attack with four hits, including a double. Jerry Mulvain scored five runs on a triple, a single and three walks and Hines and Dick Highland each had two hits. Hines once again turned in a fielding gem with a running, leaping one-handed catch of a line drive beyond the light pole in center field.

Wilke returned on Sunday night, July 23, and tossed a seven-hitter while striking out 11 as Durand smashed Rockford's American Cabinet Co. 15-5. The game was over in the first inning, when the Merchants sent 15 men to bat and scored nine runs. Wilke, Lloyd Mulvain and Jack Yaun each had two hits.

As July wound down, the Gazette also covered lots of other news. It announced the appointment of a new pastor for the Methodist Church, the Rev. John J. Main, who came to Durand from Marion, Ind., where he had been teaching in the Divinity School of Marion College for the past seven years. Carl Nuss, the manager of the new Hartman's Market, reported that more than 300 visitors attended the grand opening and several prizes were awarded, including two frying chickens to Mrs. John Walsh and a boneless rolled ham to Robert Vander Hayden. In 4-H news, brothers Dave and Ed Walsh entertained the Otter Creek Beef Club with Ed talking about how to protect calves from insects.

The biggest news of the month, though, might have been a paragraph under the headline "MERCHANTS GET WRITE-UP IN REGISTER -REPUBLIC :"

> "Dick Day, sports editor of the Rockford Register-Republic, gave the Durand Merchants a well-deserved mention in his column, Taking Time Out, in last Thursday's paper. Day listed the Merchants' record for this and last year and gave special mention to the pitching feats of both Wayne Barron and Roy Wilke."

To be mentioned in the big city daily afternoon newspaper was a special kind of validation for the Merchants. Such recognition by a Rockford paper was overdue, according to the buzz in Bill the Barber's shop. Since the Merchants had beaten several Rockford teams, the Rockford papers should acknowledge them, most of the patrons thought. But, as it turned out, the "write-up" wasn't quite what it seemed. It was simply a letter written to Day about the Merchants by none other than Buzz Stauffer:

> "Out of the mailbag... 'We townspeople of Durand,' writes Charles 'Buzz' Stauffer, 'are pretty proud of our softball team, the Durand Merchants.
>
> 'Up to now the Merchants have won 18 games while losing only 5. Their competition has been of the highest caliber, including many of your strongest Rockford teams and top outfits from both Freeport and Beloit.

'Our pitcher, Roy Wilke, whom we regard as nothing short of sensational, has lost but two of 15 games this season. In his two losing efforts, Wilke gave up only nine hits. He has pitched a no-hitter in each of the past three years. He has averaged 11 strikeouts per game this year and has an earned run average of 1.80.

'His teammate, Wayne Barron, who gave up pitching two years ago in order to play outfield, had returned to mound duties, and in his two starts defeated Smith Oil of Rockford, 2-1, on just two hits, and Freeport's Lincoln-Mercury team 17-2 on a one-hitter. '

'We have one of the finest ball parks in this area, complete with excellent lighting and loudspeaker.'

"It's also complete with some redhot fans, apparently. Durand won 34 of 40 last year, so no wonder."

Thus, the objective, detached reporter Stauffer had become a cheerleader. Mostly, however, it was evidence of how much the Merchants meant not only to Stauffer but to the entire town. They had put Durand on the map.

The Merchants wound up July by splitting a pair of games. Barron made his third start of the year and pitched a four-hitter, shutting out an outstanding B & H Tap team of Rochelle 4-0 for Durand's 20th win of the season. Barron now had given up only seven hits in three games. Lloyd Mulvain and Hines provided the power, with Mulvain hitting a two-run home run and Hines a two-run double.

Wilke, still nursing a sore arm, returned on Friday night, July 28, and hooked up in a pitching duel with Rockford Greenlee's Rosie Rosenke. Each held the other team to only one hit. Unfortunately, Wilke's one hit was a third inning home run given up to Beloit College star Sour Anderson. It cost Durand the game, 1-0, its sixth loss. Rosenke and Wilke each struck out eight; Rosenke walked two and Wilke none. The overflow crowd gave Wilke tremendous ovations when twice he registered strikeouts after three-ball, no-strike counts on Greenlee hitters.

The Merchants then lost a rare second game in a row, falling 8-3 to a surprisingly strong St. John's Church team from Rockford. Barron, winner of his last three starts, simply didn't have it and gave up five runs before manager Chuck Tracy called in Wilke with the bases loaded and no outs in the fourth inning. Wilke escaped after giving up two more runs and in the final innings gave up only one run and one hit while striking out 10. But it was too late. The Merchants couldn't do much against Danny Tighe, St. John's clever pitcher, who mixed a sneaky curve and hanging slow ball with deadly control.

Wilke stopped the two-game losing streak by pitching his second no-hitter of the season, a near-perfect game, on Friday, Aug. 4. He faced only 22 batters, giving up one walk and striking out nine, in a seven-inning 8-0 victory against the Twin Grove All Stars, a good team leading its own league with a 6-1 record. Adleman and Hartman each had two hits and Figi smashed a three-run home run.

The Merchants then did what it had never done before — it lost the third of its last four games. In a ragged affair in which Durand made five errors, Wilke caused plenty of problems of his own by walking eight in losing to Beloit's Doner's Market, 7-4, a team the Merchants had beaten 5-1 earlier in the season. Durand had only five hits, one of them a home run by Barron. The Merchants now stood at 21-8 for the season.

Durand rebounded on Wednesday night, Aug. 9, when Barron pitched a three-hitter, striking out eight and walking no one, in defeating Rockford's Bell Telephone 10-1. It was Barron's fourth win against one loss. Durand only collected four hits but was aided by four Bell errors and seven walks. Adleman led Durand hitters with a two-run home run in the second inning, all that was needed for the victory.

And then came the Merchants' fourth loss in six games, despite a one-hitter by Wilke, who dropped his second one-hitter of the season. Taking advantage of six Durand errors, Rockford's Barber-Coleman defeated the Merchants 4-0. It was the first time in two years that the Merchants had been beaten twice by the same team, Barber-Coleman having won a 3-1 game in June.

The last four losses were of some concern for the patrons of Bill the Barber because the Merchants were to face the tough Charlie Long and Parker Sporting Goods the following week. The Rockford team had already shut out Durand 8-0 earlier in June but it was against Barron.

Most of Bill the Barber's customers expected Wilke to even the score.

On Wednesday, Aug. 16, Barron pitched another gem, a three-hitter, as the Merchants got back to their winning ways by beating Rockford's Globe Imperial Association 10-4. Home runs by Hines, Dick Highland and Jack Yaun gave Durand an 8-0 lead after two innings and essentially ended the game. Hines and Highland each had two hits.

A huge crowd attending Friday night's "game of the year" against Parker Sporting Goods was disappointed because once again Wilke was on the sidelines with a sore arm. But with Barron filling in, the game was a thriller for the first four innings, when Barron matched Charlie Long in a 0-0 duel. But the duel fizzled in the fifth inning when Parker's scored five runs after two were out on four walks by Barron and two hits. Any hope of a comeback evaporated the next inning when Parker's added four more runs on three Durand errors, another walk and a single. Doubles by Adleman and Highland were the Merchants' only hits off Long. Parker's won 10-0, making it the second team of the year to beat Durand twice in the same season. In two games against the Merchants, Long pitched 14 scoreless innings and gave up only three hits. The loss was the fifth in the last eight games for the Merchants and dropped their season record to 23-10.

The comeback on Sunday night, Aug. 20, was well worth the wait. Wilke returned with a vengeance and hurled his third no-hitter of the season and fifth of his career, this time against a good Winnebago team. Stauffer dusted off the adjectives:

"If the score is 8-0, chances are that Roy Wilke pitched another no-hitter!

"The Merchants' magnificent moundsman counted his third no-hit, no-run game of the season — all of them by 8-0 finals — Sunday night against a strong, fiery Winnebago Legion team which had lost only four of 18 games before meeting up with the Merchants' great speedballer.

"Wilke, who was pitching with a rare full week's rest, struck out 13 and walked only four. He was in trouble just once — in the final inning — when a walk and an error put runners on second and third with none out. Wilke eased the situation somewhat by striking out Winnebago's top slugger, Johnny Young, but lost Leden on a three-two pitch to load the bases.

"With the pressure on, Wilke then brought the tremendous crowd to their feet by striking out Weerda on four pitched balls and whiffing Korf on another four pitches to end the game and complete the masterpiece.

"The Merchants, meanwhile, were as hot at the plate as Wilke was on the mound. They pounded an old nemesis, Russ Stringer, for 10 hits, including a 5-run, 5-hit second inning.

"Jerry Mulvain, the Merchants' agile backstop, paced the hitters with two singles and a double, while Lloyd Mulvain, Johnny Hartman and Jack Yaun each pounded a pair of safeties."

The no-hitter wasn't the biggest news of the month. The Gazette published a large architect's drawing of the proposed new elementary school building on West South Street across from the high school. The new elementary school was still two years away from opening. The school district, combined with area districts to form Community Unit School District 322 a year earlier, also announced the appointment of teachers in all its one-room school houses. Also named again to teach commerce at the high school was Bill Huddleston, who was returning after being gone all summer. Meanwhile, a tragic auto accident two miles east of town on Highway 75 at what was known as "death curve" left three men — two from Iowa and one from Wisconsin — dead. In happier news, left fielder Fred Geiser and manager Chuck Tracy, who were terrific bowlers, received their American Bowling Congress awards for the season's highest series and highest game, respectively. They were among the first inductees into the Durand Bowling Association Hall of Fame, which was created in 1978.

For the Merchants, the bad news was that they had lost their 10th game of the season. The good news was that they would not lose again. They won their 25th game in an easy 8-2 victory over Rockford Atwood, which could muster only seven players. So Merchants Jack McMahon caught and Gene Cook patrolled left field for Atwood. Each got two hits off Wilke, who spent most of the game throwing at an easy pace. Wilke then avenged an earlier 1-0 defeat by pitching a four-hitter and beating Rockford Greenlee and Rosie Rosenke 5-3. Hartman paced Durand hitters with a three-run home run in the first inning in the Merchants' 26th win.

Cold weather in early September cut into the Merchants' schedule and held them to only four games for the month. They opened the month with an 8-5 victory over Irish Grove and its one-armed pitcher, Vern Simmer. Wilke pitched a five-hitter and struck out 10 as Adleman with a pair of doubles and a single, Hartman with a two-run homer and a double, and Hines with a double and a single led Durand's hitters.

The Merchants chalked up their 28th victory of the year on Sept. 6 with an 11-3 decision over the Rock County (Wis.) Farm Bureau team. Barron registered the win and Jerry Mulvain paced Durand's hitters with two doubles. On Sunday night, Sept. 17, Huddleston made his first appearance since May 26 and pitched a three-hitter, beating a good Ridott team and Johnnie Smith, who eventually would pitch for Durand, 10-3. Adleman led all hitters with a home run and a double.

The final game of the season was announced for the following Sunday, Sept. 23, as a benefit for Beverly Geiser, the wife of Merchant left fielder Fred Geiser. Beverly, who was the catcher for the Durand women's softball team, had been stricken with poliomyelitis a week earlier and was still in St. Anthony Hospital in Rockford. Polio was one of the most dreaded diseases of the time. Just five years earlier, in 1945, summer vacation for school children in Durand was extended two weeks because of a polio scare. Classes began on Sept. 17 with a nurse on duty. Polio and its unrelenting attack on a Durand family in 1955 would become the biggest national story in the town's history.

A large and chilled crowd turned out for the final game of 1950 and was rewarded with a thrilling 3-2 victory over Rock City. Both Wilke and Huddleston pitched against the talented Marv Neidermeier for Rock City. Rock City scored in the first inning but the Merchants tied it up at 1-1 in the third inning on a run-scoring double by Dick Highland. Wilke pitched shutout ball in the second, third and fourth innings and Huddleston took over in the fifth. Rock City scored in the sixth on a triple and a single and took a 2-1 lead. Down to its last three outs, Barron led off the seventh for Durand with a single and scored on an error with the tying run. Jerry Mulvain singled and Adleman was safe on a fielder's choice, loading the bases. Highland's ground ball to shortstop then scored the winning run. The benefit was a huge success; more than $100 was raised for Beverly Geiser's fight against polio.

The year was marked by the beginning of the Korean War when North Korea launched an attack beyond the 38th parallel into South Korea on June 25. Gen. Douglas MacArthur, at age 70, was appointed commander of U.N. forces in Korea and in early August the U.S. Army called up more than 60,000 enlisted reservists for active duty. President Truman avoided calling the conflict a war, labeling it a "police action." In baseball, the Cubs improved slightly, finishing in seventh place instead of eighth with a 64-89 record. The New York Yankees, led by Joe DiMaggio and Yogi Berra, swept the Philadelphia Phillies four games to none in the World Series. The Rockford Peaches won their third women's league baseball championship with a 67-44 record and fourth playoff championship.

And the Merchants completed another outstanding season. It was the first year of extensive coverage of the team by the Gazette, which reported on 37 of the 40 games. Although Durand's 30-10 record was not as good on the face of it as 1949's 34-6, it could be considered slightly better because of the higher quality of the competition. The Merchants posted at least a 16-4 record against the best Rockford teams. Wilke once again led Durand pitchers with a 21-6 record. His combined 1949-50 mark stood at 52 wins and 12 losses. Barron finished the year at 6-2, Huddleston was 3-0 and Figi was 0-2. After two years, it was apparent that Adleman and the Mulvain brothers were the best hitters, a notch above Dick Highland, Joe Hines and Johnny Hartman, each very good hitters in their own right. Adleman hit at least eight home runs in 1950, followed by four by Hines and three by Highland. The Merchants two-year record was 64 wins and 16 losses, better than nearly all area teams, none of which played as difficult a schedule. With Wilke only 25 years old and the possibility of Huddleston giving him some relief, the Merchants' future looked even brighter.

Catcher Jerry Mulvain, left, pitcher Roy Wilke, center, and manager Chuck Tracy. This photo appeared in The Durand Gazette on Aug. 20, 1950, after Wilke pitched a no-hitter against Winnebago, winning 8-0. (Photo courtesy of Judy Wilke).

From left: Carl Nuss, Charles "Buzz" Stauffer, Ralph Kehm and Merchants' manager Chuck Tracy playing pinochle at Nuss' home on Center Street. Nuss served as an umpire and scorekeeper at some Merchants' games. Stauffer was The Durand Gazette's reporter who covered the team. (Photo courtesy of Carl's son, Gary Nuss).

Roy and Betty Wilke in a photo taken in the backyard of the home on West Howard Street of Betty's mother and my grandmother, Olive Amundsen. (Photo courtesy of Sharon Place).

Bill Huddleston's photo from the 1951 yearbook of Durand High School, where he taught business classes. Huddleston was an excellent pitcher, faster than and nearly as good as Roy Wilke. But he pitched for the Merchants in parts of only two seasons, in 1950 and 1951, before moving from Durand.

Wayne and Lois Adleman on their 65th wedding anniversary on Sept. 4, 2005. (Photo courtesy of Wayne Adleman).

Jerry and Juanita Mulvain outside their home on West North Street on June 10, 2007. (Photo taken by Mike Waller).

Durand's elementary school, on the left, and the high school, on the right, on West South Street. The elementary school opened in 1952 and the high school opened in 1958. My class was the first one to graduate from it, in 1959. (Photo courtesy of Helen C. Johnson).

Durand's "old" high school, across West South Street from the new one. It also contained the junior high school, on the left. (Photo courtesy of Helen C. Johnson).

The original Durand public school, built in 1888 on State Street. (Photo courtesy of Norm Chilton).

The Durand public school in the 1940s. It was converted to the American Legion Hall in 1952, when the new elementary school opened on West South Street. (Photo courtesy of Norm Chilton).

CHAPTER 5

A Lost Season

The promise of another great Merchants season in 1951 wilted before the first game was played. The Merchants' ace pitcher, Roy Wilke, would be out for the year with a sore arm.

Another shocker came from the Gazette, which for some undisclosed reason decided not to cover any of the Merchants' games. The paper reported only four scores with no details throughout the entire season — two victories the second week in June and two more in the middle of July. The only other Merchants' story in 1951 appeared on Aug. 9 when the paper announced that three benefit games had been scheduled for later in August — one to help the village defray expenses for its annual DDT spraying, one to benefit the Red Cross and the third to assist Wilke with his recent surgery, the details of which were not disclosed. But the Gazette never reported on any of the three games or how much money was raised.

No explanation was offered for these daffy decisions by the Gazette. It may simply be that reporter Charles "Buzz" Stauffer was absent the entire summer and owner-editor John R. Van Sickle displayed his lack of sympathy for sports by not assigning anyone to report on the games. No matter the reason, when it came to determining what readers wanted and the significance of the team to the town, Van Sickle still had a tin ear.

Jerry Mulvain thought 1951 was the third straight year that the Merchants played about 40 games. The pitchers replacing Wilke included Wayne "Red" Barron, Bill Huddleston, Bernie Figi and Johnnie Smith in his first season for Durand. Mulvain believed Durand won about 30 games again. That seems unlikely with Wilke on the sidelines the entire year. But a record of 27 wins and 13 losses seems plausible. At that rate, the Merchants' three-year record would have climbed to 91 wins and 29 losses.

The Gazette did report on about 10 games played by the Durand women's softball team that was coached by Jerry Mulvain (he coached the women's team for more than 20 years). In some game stories, the lineup was listed and featured Beverly Geiser at catcher, Ruth Miller at pitcher, Dorothy McKearn at first base, Gertrude Buerkle at second base, Marjorie Dittmar at shortstop, Marilyn Place at third base, Dorothy Hartman in left field, Maxine Michaelis in center field and Marian Walsh in right field. Reserves included Joyce Stockdale, Shirley Bartelt, S. Nath, P. Polukey and L. Nyman.

As far as I was concerned, the biggest news of 1951 was the sudden death on June 28 of my grandmother, Margaret Waller, at age 74. She had been married 50 years to my grandfather, Lloyd Waller, and was survived by three sons — my dad Daniel Ward Waller, Everett "Doc" Waller and Howard "Bud" Waller. It was my first encounter with death and the suddenness of it left me wondering what it all meant. She lived on West Main Street just two houses from my buddy Bill Haggerty. Nearly every day during the summers Bill and I stopped by her home for homemade cookies and then scooted across the alley to load up on more sweets from Grandma Dailey, Bill's grandmother.

Stauffer was back on the job in 1952 and announced in a Gazette story on May 1 the first Merchants' practice of the season. Returning were Wilke and many other veterans, including Jack Sharp and Johnnie Smith, both Merchant rookies in 1951. However, missing from the roster were second baseman Johnny Hartman and outfielder Jack Yaun, who were serving with the Army in Korea, and first baseman Dick Highland and pitcher Bill Huddleston, neither of whom played for the Merchants after 1951.

Highland retired and Huddleston accepted a teaching position elsewhere. Red Barron also was missing; he was undergoing treatments at Chicago's Hines Hospital for a back ailment.

Despite losing several veterans, the Merchants opened the season on Sunday night, May 18, on a winning note. The year's layoff didn't affect Wilke; he hurled a four-hitter and struck out 10 as the Merchants defeated Rockford's Nyland Tool Co. 12-4. Wilke drew a big ovation from the large crowd when he struck out the side in the fourth inning. Third baseman Sharp led Durand hitters with a perfect three for three. First baseman Vernal Jones, an aged newcomer (he was 39 years old) from Avon, Wis., had a pair of doubles and center fielder Bernie Figi also had two hits.

Wilke was not as sharp the next week as he and the Merchants lost a dispute-ridden game to Rockford's Barber-Coleman, 10-9, and evened their record to 1-1. Durand sent the game into extra innings on a two-run double by Figi, who was tagged out between second and third base on a disputed "time out" mix-up to end the rally in the bottom of the seventh inning. The story failed to explain the "time out" mix-up. Barber-Coleman scored two runs on four hits in the eighth inning and then withstood another rally by Durand when shortstop Wayne Adleman was robbed by the center fielder of a second home run to end the game. Joe Hines had three hits and Jones, Sharp, Figi and Charlie Buss, a rookie who sometimes replaced Johnny Hartman at second base or patrolled right field, each had two.

The Merchants donned their hitting clothes the next week and slammed 49 hits and scored 43 runs in crushing Rock City 20-0 and Dakota 23-3. Wilke pitched a two-hitter and struck out nine against Rock City on Wednesday night, May 28. Lloyd Mulvain, who had taken over the job of manager, paced Durand hitters with five hits, including a home run and a double. Buss had four hits, including two doubles, and Jones had a triple and two doubles. In all, the Merchants had 26 hits. On Sunday night, Durand banged out 23 hits against Dakota, led by Sharp's four hits, including three home runs. Figi had two triples and a single and Wilke also had three hits in a game in which he mostly lobbed the ball to hitters after Durand took a 10-run lead in the first two innings. Sharp's three home runs thrilled the crowd but not as much as two Durand pinch hitters, according to Stauffer:

"The crowd, one of the largest of the early season, reserved their biggest applause for the pinch-hitting appearances of youngsters Ronnie Adleman and Mickey Mulvain, who batted for their dads, Wayne and Lloyd. In the sixth, Ronnie grounded out in his first trip and lined out in his second appearance while Mickey poked a single over the shortstop's head and scored a few minutes later on Sharp's home run. The little fellows, neither of whom stand much taller than a bat, then took over second and third base during the final inning, although neither of them had a fielding opportunity."

Wayne Adleman and Jerry Mulvain, Mike Mulvain's uncle (Mike's dad Lloyd died in 1956), don't remember the two boys pinch-hitting for their fathers. Nor does Mike, who would have been 8 years old. Ron Adleman, who also would have been 8 years old, could not be reached.

The Merchants returned to tough competition the next week and won both games, extending their winning streak to four and season record to 5-1. First, Wilke came through in the clutch as Durand beat a good Beloit Muni Electric team 6-5. Wilke gave up three hits and three runs in the first inning, then settled down and pitched well the rest of the game. His worst jam came in the fifth inning, when a hit and two walks loaded the bases with none out for Beloit. One run scored on a long fly ball, but Wilke squelched the rally by getting the next two hitters on pop-ups. Beloit, down one run, threatened again in the seventh and last inning by scratching out two hits. But Wilke once again shut the door by striking out the final hitter. Jack McMahon, who had last played for the Merchants in 1950, led Durand hitters with a two-run double. Figi, Jerry Mulvain and Jones each had singles.

Johnnie Smith made his season's pitching debut on Sunday night, holding the 755th Air Force Squadron from Delevan, Wis., to three hits in five innings as Durand won 5-1. Smith struck out nine before being relieved the last two innings by Wilke. Sharp had his third perfect night of the season with three hits in three plate appearances, including another home run and a double. Fred Geiser, Joe Hines and Wilke each chipped in with one hit.

The return of McMahon was a remarkable story in itself. McMahon, who at the age of 16 in 1949 became the youngest Merchant ever to play, moved in 1950 to Corpus Christi, Tex., to complete his senior year of high school. As a pitcher for his high school team, he won four games and lost one. He also played outfield, second base and shortstop. If McMahon was not the best baseball player ever to come from Durand, he surely was in the top three. Perhaps the Mulvain brothers were better, but neither ever tried his hand at professional baseball. Only three Durand players ever did — McMahon and two of his Durand High School contemporaries, Bob Adleman and Jim Sweet. Adleman was an infielder and after attending several major league tryout camps wound up playing part of a year for the Mattoon (Ill.) Indians, a Class D team in the Mississippi-Ohio Valley League. Sweet, a pitcher, also went to several tryout camps and signed on with the Janesville (Wis.) Cubs, a Class D team in the Wisconsin State League. Neither Adleman nor Sweet ever advanced beyond Class D.

But McMahon was the most talented of the three and despite his reputation of displaying less than good judgment on occasion was a surer bet to go far in professional baseball. He was a cocky ballplayer. But as the great pitcher Dizzy Dean said, "If you can do it, it ain't bragging." And McMahon could do it. He was the kind of player who would announce in the batter's box that he was going to bunt. And then he bunted, and with his great speed embarrassed the opposing team by beating it out for an infield single. In 1951 McMahon seemed well on his way. He signed a contract with the Corpus Christi Aces, a Class B team in the Gulf Coast League, and was optioned to the Odessa Oilers, a Class C Team in the Longhorn League. After that, he played for some other minor league teams but it's not clear which ones. Nor is it clear how high he advanced in the minor leagues. How he ended his career is less fuzzy.

Bill the Barber, who always said that McMahon "had a million dollars worth of talent and a 10-cent head," said that he knew exactly how McMahon's baseball career turned out because McMahon himself told Bill this story:

"Jack was playing well as the shortstop for the Class B team in

Roanoke, Va., I think. He decided he wanted to buy a new car so he met one day after a game with the manager and general manager. He demanded a $400 raise and said he would quit if he didn't get it. They told him to close the door on his way out. And then they blackballed him — he never played professional baseball again."

In fact, major league baseball owners totally controlled all players in the 1950s and it's not hard to imagine that more than a few had their careers strangled when they angered the powers-that-were. It's impossible to say whether McMahon was telling Bill the Barber the truth. But one thing is true: Despite McMahon's great talent, there is no record that he played professional baseball after 1951.

The Merchants ran their winning streak to six straight by beating Podunk College 7-1 on Wednesday night, June 11, and Rockford's Salamone & Son 8-7 in an extra-inning affair on Sunday night, June 15. Wilke pitched "a 14-karat mound masterpiece" against Podunk, limiting the Rockford school to three hits while striking out 10. Sharp continued his blistering hitting streak, pounding out three hits, including a two-run home run. Jerry Mulvain also had three hits. An overflow crowd watched the Merchants come from behind three times to edge Salamone in nine innings. Durand fell behind 3-0 in the second inning but tied the game in the third inning with three runs of its own on hits by Adleman and Jerry Mulvain. Wilke ran into control trouble in the sixth inning when Salamone scored three more runs on two walks, an error and a passed ball. Smith relieved Wilke and ended the rally with a fly-ball out. Durand tied the game once again with three runs in the bottom of the seventh, the big blow being Sharp's two-run single. The Merchants fell behind a third time in the eighth inning when Salamone capitalized on a walk and a long fly ball to take a 7-6 lead. But singles by Smith and Adleman tied it again in the bottom of the eighth. Durand won the game 8-7 when Hines walked with the bases loaded in the bottom of the ninth. After the first eight games of the season, Sharp had exploded for at least 16 hits, including four home runs. It was beginning to be obvious that he was as good a hitter as Adleman and the

Mulvain brothers.

The winning streak ended the following week when Sharp substituted on the mound for Wilke and Smith. Sharp pitched a five-hitter but his teammates got only two hits, singles by Adleman and Jerry Mulvain, in a 2-1 loss to Carter-Gruenewald of Juda, Wis. Fred Geiser made a spectacular catch in the seventh inning when he snagged a foul ball between cars parked along the left field line.

For many of us members of the Foul Ball Brigade, faithfully chasing down mishit balls each week for a nickel apiece, the big news was the announcement in the Gazette of Durand's first Little League baseball team for boys between the ages of 9 and 12. It was perfect timing — I was 10 years old and raring to go. Better yet, three coaches were named for the new team, all of them Merchant players — Lloyd Mulvain, Wayne Adleman and Don Hubbartt. Other teams in Pecatonica, Davis and Dakota were being established and with Durand would form a league. Durand's first practice was scheduled for Thursday, June 26.

The Merchants dropped their third game of the season on June 21 when they were held to only four hits — two of them by Wilke — in a 7-3 loss to Rockford Broadway AC. Wilke pitched fairly well before a large and sweltering crowd but two errors and a couple of extra-base hits put Durand behind early and for good. The highlight of the game came when Benny Rinaldo, one of the best pitchers in the region, hurled the final three innings for Broadway AC. He dazzled the crowd with his "phenomenal speed and sharp breaking hooks," though he didn't strike out anyone.

Durand recovered on the following Sunday, June 25, and defeated the 755th Air Force Squadron from Delavan, Wis., 7-6, for the second time in three weeks in a game played "before 300 fans and 30,000 mosquitos." Smith, who was sailing along with a 6-4 lead and a six-hitter, suddenly lost his control in the seventh inning and Wilke was called to the rescue. But he gave up a double and two runs before snuffing the rally. Vernal Jones ended the game in the bottom of the seventh with a run-scoring double, giving the Merchants an 8-3 season record.

Beloit Muni Electric returned to Legion Field the following Sunday for the second time in a month and avenged its earlier loss to the Merchants. Wilke gave up a three-run home run and fell behind 4-0 in the first two innings and the Merchants couldn't recover, losing 6-5.

Durand improved its record to 9-4 on Sunday, July 13, when it smoked the Rockford Firemen 10-1 at Legion Field. Wilke held the firemen to two scratch hits and struck out eight. The game story was notable in that it featured for the first time a partial box score showing how Merchant hitters fared. Adleman, who played second base, Sharp, Lloyd Mulvain and Hines each had two hits.

Less than one month after heralding the formation of Durand's first Little League team, the young boys played their first game on Wednesday night, July 9, and the Gazette story, most likely written by Stauffer, appeared under the account of the Merchants' victory over the firemen with the headline:

> "Little Leaguers Lose, 6-3, In Opener With Davis:" "Durand's Little Leaguers — youngsters between 9 and 12 — dropped their opening game of the year Wednesday night at Legion Field in a 6-3 decision to the Davis Little Leaguers.
>
> "A large and enthusiastic crowd found themselves surprised and delighted at the brand of baseball exhibited by the kids. Durand's pitcher, lefty Dick Sweet, chalked up 10 strikeouts and teammate Mike Waller, who played a stellar game at shortstop, paced the hitters with three for four, including a perfect bunt."

Thus began my career as a ballplayer, wearing a Merchants' red-and-black uniform made by my mother.

The Merchants ran their winning streak to three the next week by avenging losses earlier in the season to Rockford Broadway AC and Carter-Gruenewald of Juda, Wis. Partial box scores were published for both games. With Wilke sidelined by a sore arm, Smith pitched a three-hitter as Durand defeated Broadway's Rosie Rosenke 11-2. Sharp and Figi each had two hits. Wilke returned to face the Juda team on Sunday night, July 20, but was hit hard for three runs in the first inning and two more in the fourth. Sharp pitched the final three innings and gave up only one hit as Durand won, 9-5. Sharp also broke a 5-5 tie in the fourth inning with a grand-slam home run. The game lost a lot of its luster when Juda showed up short-handed by three players. Smith took over pitching chores for the visitors and Figi and Ray Michaelis filled out Juda's lineup so that Sunday's crowd would see a game. Adleman, again playing second base, led Durand with three hits and Sharp added two.

Sharp continued his pitching and hot hitting the following week by leading the Merchants to its fourth straight victory and 12th in 16 games. He gave up nine hits but only one in the last four innings and managed to register a 6-5 decision over Podunk College, the second Durand victory of the season over Podunk. Adleman, back at third base with Sharp pitching, rapped out three hits and Sharp and Buss each had two, according to the box score. Ken Ditzler, who would enter his senior year at Durand High School in the fall, made his first and only appearance in 1952 for the Merchants.

The winning streak reached five on Wednesday night, Aug. 6, as a ninth-inning single by Jerry Mulvain gave the Merchants an exciting 12-11 win over Freeport's Micro-Switch. The Merchants, behind 6-4 in the last half of the sixth inning, scored seven runs on six hits and a pair of errors to apparently ice the game at 11-6. But poor Durand fielding opened the door for Mico-Switch in the top of the seventh and Freeport tied the game with five runs. Both Wilke and Smith pitched, but the Gazette story did not offer any details about their performance. Jerry Mulvain lead Durand with four hits, Hines had three and Adleman, Figi and Hubbartt, playing first base, each had two. The story was accompanied with a partial box score, the last one to appear in 1952. It remains a mystery as to why box scores for only five straight games were published that season, especially since the Gazette nearly always printed box scores for Durand High School baseball games.

Durand won two more games in the next week, with Wilke giving up only one run in 13 innings, and boosted its season record to 15-4. But the Gazette only reported that Wilke pitched well and didn't offer any other details. The Merchants ran their winning streak to eight the following week as Smith tossed a two-hitter and defeated Rockford's

American Cabinet 3-1 on Wednesday night, Aug. 27. The game featured four great defensive plays by Durand. Third baseman Sharp dove at a line drive between third and shortstop, knocked it down and threw out the runner at first while lying flat on his back. Veteran observers rated the play as one of the best ever made at Legion Field. Other outstanding plays were made by shortstop Adleman, who twice raced far behind his position to pull down potential hits, and Fred Geiser, whose letter perfect throw to the plate from center field cut down an American Cabinet runner in the second inning.

At the same time, the Gazette reported a big news story from the Waller household:

> "Billy Haggerty suffered a compound fracture of his left arm while playing at the Ward Waller country home last Friday afternoon.
>
> "He was taken to the Swedish-American Hospital, Rockford, where the fracture was reduced. Both bones below his elbow were broken. He and his cousin, Francis Cirrincione, were spending the day at the Waller home."

The story read as if we were a family of some means, owning a country home. In fact, the country home was a former one-room schoolhouse named Fenlon School four miles north of Durand that my dad bought for a few hundred dollars. He moved us all there for a year while he and carpenter Oscar "Curley" Weaver remodeled our house in town. The renovation would include our first indoor plumbing. The story didn't offer many details of Bill's accident, but it occurred when he fell out of a tree we were climbing at the back of the property, renamed Happy Half-Acre by my dad, on which the schoolhouse was located. My mother did not know how to drive but somehow got access to a car with a standard shift. We all climbed into the car and, lurching forward in fits and starts as my mother tried to operate the clutch, finally made it to town. The Haggertys then drove Bill to the hospital.

That wasn't the only Waller news of the week. The Gazette reported that my dad, Ward Waller, attended a meeting of the Illinois Rural Letter Carriers Association at Hotel Sherman in Chicago and was elected a member of the executive committee of the state board. He served on that committee for several years while he was the director of the Blue Cross-Blue Shield program for the carriers' association and eventually became president of the association.

He joined the Durand Post Office as postmaster in 1936, the same year he married my mother and Floyd "Bump" Sarver began delivering mail on Rural Route #2. In August 1942 Dad took over Rural Route #1, succeeding Ralph Hoyt, who retired. Emogene Dailey was named acting postmaster and Mrs. Lillie Doyle became her assistant. A few years later Mrs. Doyle became the postmaster. Dad served 29 years on Route #1 before retiring and Bump, who umpired some of the Merchants' games and was the official scorekeeper at others, retired after 46 years.

Dad delivered mail to 235 customers over 54 miles six days a week. At Christmas time, it was a treat for me and my brothers and sister to take turns riding in the back seat of his car as he delivered the mail and picked up dozens of Christmas presents. They ranged from homemade cookies, pork chops and small steaks to cake, cigarettes and wine.

He was very active in the community, where he lived all of his 92 years. He was a charter member of the Durand Lions Club in 1936, was named chairman of the United War Chest and Community fund drive for the town, was president of the Durand School Board in 1954, president of the Durand Centennial Celebration in 1956, chairman of lay lectors for several years at St. Mary's Catholic Church and the village clerk from 1971 to 1977. He spent most of his life cheerleading for Durand, repeating his favorite mantra: "Life is grand when you live in Durand." Durand thought he was grand, too, and named him and Gladys Bliss, owner of Bliss Grocery, the village's first Citizens of the Year in 1976. Four years later, Bump Sarver was named Citizen of the Year.

On the softball diamond, the Merchants' winning streak ended abruptly at the end of August with two straight losses to the same team, Winnebago. The first was an 8-7 heartbreaking defeat to Rosie Rosenke, who was recruited by Winnebago from his Rockford team, and came in the first round of the Rockton Invitational Tournament in which Durand was one of the favorites to win. Wilke pitched a four-hitter and the Merchants pounded out nine hits. But five errors and three costly decisions by the umpires spelled the difference. One of the decisions came in the sixth inning after the Merchants scored two runs and Adleman was about to score the tying run but was called out at home plate. According to Stauffer, "The crowd booed lustily for his apparent miss-call." Sharp and Jones paced Durand with three hits each, including home runs. Jerry Mulvain added two singles.

Five days later, on Tuesday, Sept. 2, the Merchants lost again to Winnebago, this time 3-2 in extra innings at Legion Field. Wilke hooked up in a pitching duel with Russ Stringer before Winnebago scored the winning run in the top of the eighth inning. Jerry Mulvain led Durand with two hits. The game was somewhat tainted because neither team had a full compliment of players, which happened on occasion. The solution was to recruit players on the spot so the large crowd could see a game. What was unusual this time was that women players were recruited to fill out the lineups. Stauffer reported that Bev Geiser and Marilyn Place shared right field duty for the Merchants and Winnebago "played a smooth fielding gal first-baseman, Allen, to complete their lineup."

Durand rebounded on Sunday, Sept. 7, by crushing Rockford's Globe Imperial, 15-2, and running its season record to 17-6. Wilke pitched a three-hitter at Legion Field but lost his shutout in the fifth inning when he tumbled into a streak of wildness and walked five hitters. Sharp with a home run and a single and Jerry Mulvain with a double and a single led the Durand attack.

The Merchants wound up their season a week later at Legion Field on Sunday, Sept. 14, with a 14-0 romp over Evansville, Wis., in 50-degree weather. Smith came within a whisker of a no-hitter, giving up only an infield single in the fourth inning. Jones led the Durand hit parade with four hits, including two home runs, and seven RBIs. Adleman had three singles, Hines a pair of triples and Wilke a triple and a single.

The year was marked by the election of Republicans Dwight D. Eisenhower as president and Richard M. Nixon as vice president. They defeated Democrats Gov. Adlai Stevenson of Illinois and Sen. Estes Kefauver of Tennessee. Rocky Marciano knocked out Jersey Joe Walcott in the 13th round to win the heavyweight boxing championship of the world. In baseball, the Cubs posted their best record in six years. Led by left fielder Hank Sauer's 37 home runs and 121 RBIs, they finished in fifth place with a 77-77 mark. The New York Yankees, paced by sluggers Mickey Mantle and Johnny Mize and pitchers Allie Reynolds and Vic Raschi, won their fourth straight World Series by defeating the Brooklyn Dodgers four games to three. The Rockford Peaches won slightly more than half of their games in the All-American Girls Professional Baseball League and finished in third place with a 55-54 record.

And the Merchants completed another terrific season even though they reduced the number of games played to an average of two a week instead of the three a week in the previous three years. Against top-flight competition, they finished with an 18-6 record and were 11-2 against teams from Rockford, Freeport and Beloit. Wilke won 11 games and lost 5, bringing his three-year pitching mark to 63 wins and 17 losses, a winning record of 79 per cent. Smith was undefeated at 6-0 and Sharp finished with a 1-1 record. The Merchants' four-year mark now stood at an impressive 109 wins and 35 losses, a 75 per cent winning record. Even the great Cleveland Indians team of 1954, which posted a 111-43 record for a 71 percent winning mark, couldn't match that. Sharp was the Merchants' best hitter, banging out at least 32 hits, including seven home runs, for the season. Adleman had at least 21 hits and Jerry Mulvain and Jones each recorded at least 16 hits. The chatter at Bill the Barber's Shop during the off-season was about how long the Merchants and Yankees dynasties could last. The consensus was arrived at quickly: at least another season.

Jack Yaun, one of the Merchants' right fielders, at his post in Korea in 1951 or 1952 during the Korean War. (Photo courtesy of the Yuan family).

Jack McMahon in his Durand grade school basketball uniform in 1947. McMahon played a few softball games with the Merchants in 1949 and 1950 before signing a professional baseball contract in 1951 with the Corpus Christi Aces of the Class B Gulf Coast League. McMahon returned to the Merchants in 1952 and played a few more years.

Johnnie Smith, Merchants' pitcher, on his wedding day, July 14, 1939, in Clinton, Iowa. (Photo courtesy of his daughter, Betty Rhyner).

1958 Durand Cherubs women's softball team coached by Jerry Mulvain, at the far right in the back row. Mulvain coached Durand women softball teams for more than 20 years. He also coached women's 4-H teams for many years. Front row from left are: Bill Haggerty, my buddy and the assistant coach, Charlene Nelson, Sally Kelsey and Sue Waller. Second row, from left: Linda Nelson, Unknown, Unknown, Delores Meier, Judy Slamp, Shirley Adleman, and Kathy Kelsey. Back row, from left, Mary Chilton, Jo Ellen Walsh, Sharon Nuss, Unknown, Sue Meissen, Edna Humphrey and Bonnie Tschabold.

CHAPTER 6

The Age of Innocence

If my father's mantra of "life is grand when you live in Durand" was true, it was even more so when growing up in the village in the late 1940s and early 1950s. It was an age of innocence, a much simpler and more carefree time than today, an era before technology began advancing, improving and corrupting our lives. For many of the years it was an age without television, air conditioning, indoor plumbing in many homes, cell phones, smart phones or even private telephone lines, video games, personal computers, social media, seat belts, air bags, power steering, electric windows or baby car seats in automobiles, bottled water (we drank from the garden hose and lived to tell about it), a town movie theater or crime — no one locked their doors at night.

The last significant crime anyone could remember was in the fall of 1924 when burglars broke into the Ploetz Drug Store and stole all the fountain pens, Kodak cameras and flashlights, valued at about $150. A month later in October burglars forced their way through the front door of Axel Erickson's clothing store and stole racks of men's suits and overcoats and women's coats and dresses. Erickson estimated the loss at $1,500. No one recalls the crimes ever being solved.

Entertainment for youngsters was sports and whatever your imagination could invent. In the summers, Durand had two main organized forms of family entertainment: watching the Merchants beat up on the big city teams at Legion Field two or three nights a week and the outdoor "free show" sponsored by the local business association every Thursday night in town square park. The free show, which was started in 1937, was a particular treat. The organizers strung up a white sheet on rope between two trees in the town square park and played a movie on a 32 millimeter projector after it got dark. Everyone brought blankets to sit on to watch the night's film. Some of our favorites were cowboy movies starring Roy Rogers, Gene Autry, Lash LaRue, Randolph Scott, Hopalong Cassidy or Tom Mix. Other favorites were comedies with Bud Abbott and Lou Costello and Ma and Pa Kettle. We always waited anxiously for the intermission, when we hustled across the street to either Bliss' grocery store on the east or Bentley and Highland's grocery on the west to buy penny candy. The next day several of us returned to the park to hunt for spare change that might have fallen out of people's pockets as they watched the movie.

Most of our summer days were filled with playing baseball at Legion Field and then playing on the Little League, Pony League and American Legion baseball teams. A dozen or more of us — Bill Haggerty, Mike Mulvain, Lawrence Damon, Mo Ostergard, brothers Ron and Terry Foss, Ray Keller, Jerry Whisman, Ron Adleman, Dick Sweet, Rich Bosshart, Dennis Bliss, Dave "Red" Welch, Russ Sarver, Shirley Adleman and I — met nearly every morning at the ballpark. We all had our own gloves, balls and bats — wooden, not the aluminum ones used today. But we used Lloyd Mulvain's expensive new catcher's mitt that his son Mike usually brought each day. Its pocket was so small that you had to catch the ball perfectly or it would pop out of the glove. We chose up sides and played baseball until the noon whistle on top of the fire house sounded. We all hustled home for lunch and usually returned to the diamond in the afternoon to play ball until supper time. Or we spent the afternoon playing basketball at Whisman's, or Ron Adleman's or Shirley Adleman's driveway. Sometimes we would break into the old high school gym by sneaking though an unlocked window to play basketball.

Shirley Adleman, the youngest daughter of umpire Earl "Pete" Adleman, was a remarkable athlete and the only girl who played sports with us. She was better than most of us and as good as the best of us, whether it was baseball, basketball, football or bowling. She was Durand's greatest woman athlete but was unlucky to be born in 1942. Shirley was good enough but not old enough to play for the Rockford

Peaches in the All-American Girls Professional Baseball League, which folded in 1954. (At least three Durand High School girls, all about age 16 — Marcia Koglin, Maryellyn Lilley and Neva Wallace — tried out for the Peaches in the early 1950s but none was invited to join the team). Durand schools didn't have any women's teams during this era so Shirley missed out playing such scholastic sports as basketball, softball and volleyball. She also could have been a terrific women's college basketball player but the sport didn't become popular and widespread until long after she was past college age. She was a great bowler and sometimes teamed with Merchant left fielder Fred Geiser to win mixed doubles tournaments. In 1964, as a member of The Fords in the Durand Women's Bowling League, Shirley lead the team in a tournament in Ft. Atkinson, Wis., to a fifth place finish out of 350 entries. Her teammates were Beverly Geiser, Mary Lou Walsh, Dorothy McKearn and Carol Highbarger. Three years later, Shirley and her Ditsworth Masonry team of East Alton, won the Illinois state championship in Champaign. Shirley bowled a 608 three-game series.

She also was a star infielder and hitter for the Durand women's and 4-H softball teams. In 1965, as a member of the Alton Lakers softball team, she collect four trophies while leading Alton to the championship of the Shelbyville tournament. The trophies were for first home run, first extra base hit, most hits in the tournament and first place team.

In an interview, Shirley recalled being a member of the Merchants' Foul Ball Brigade:

> "I remember chasing foul balls and returning them to the concession stand for a whole 5 cents a ball. June (Shirley's sister, June Adleman Hardesty) remembers Dad going over to the ballpark early and mowing the outfield. Everybody wanted Dad to umpire because he was fair whether the teams were from Durand or not. He called balls and strikes the way he saw them and was excellent at it. It was his life, he loved it. As we got a little older, we joined the Durand women's softball team which Dad helped manage. One year we won every game except one against Marengo. Orville Keller owned the Hilltop Drive-Inn (a

mile south of town) and when we won a game we would go up there for a free Root Beer. Orville about went broke that year!

"Dad built the first Durand bowling alley, which had four lanes. He also was a school bus driver for 20 years and the first TV repairman in Durand. You name it and he did it.

"The Trask Bridge Picnic was a special event. Dad would drop off June and me on his way to work at Pinehurst Dairy (in Rockford) early in the morning and come back and umpire softball games there until dark. We would meet him at the ball field in the evening and ride home with him."

The picnic was an annual event that drew thousands of people to farmland adjacent to the Pecatonica River about five miles southwest of town. It was billed as the world's largest farm picnic. Shirley continued:

"At one time June was a Girl Scout leader and the Scouts wanted to earn their ice-skating badges. So Dad, who was water commissioner, and June's husband Art, decided to flood the old high school parking lot during the middle of the night. The next day, the Girl Scout troop had an ice-skating party and everyone earned their badges."

Mike Mulvain also remembered being part of the Foul Ball Brigade:

"Going to Merchants' games at Legion Field was one of the highlights of our lives while growing up in the 1950s. It was especially exciting when Roy Wilke pitched. His feared fast ball sent many batters back to the bench with three strikes. We chased down foul balls and literally risked out lives running through the maze of cars and across the streets in furious competition to retrieve the ball. Our reward was a nickel or a Popsicle. But the most important reward was for the bragging rights for who retrieved the most balls during a game. My dad would let me turn off the lights after the game. The switch was on a pole in right field and you had to pull hard and fast. Hundreds of moths had gathered around the lights and when you shut them off, they all fell to the ground. Those days were some of the most memorable in my life. They were prior to 1956 when my dad died and life was good."

Another lifelong buddy of mine, Jim Walsh, was dazzled watching the Merchant games:

"I was too young to really appreciate what a phenomenal thing was going on right in our little town. I know it was amazing to watch these guys in action. I don't know how anyone could ever hit Roy Wilke. Things were quite different then. No TV set until I was 16, no cell phones. We entertained ourselves by playing outside. Kick the can and that sort of thing. Fifteen to 20 kids playing at a time. We would stay outside till we were ready to pee our pants. The ball games at Legion Field were the biggest thing going on in town. People would come from all over. Cars everywhere. Mostly Fords and Chevies, some Plymouths. All the way down first and third base line and across the streets. There weren't a lot of bleachers. Many sat in their cars to watch the games. Lloyd Mulvain would sometimes let me go to right field and flip on the switch for the lights. He always warned me to push the lever up fast and hard to eliminate any arcing of the contacts. If you thought the plate umpire was not calling balls and strikes correctly, you could stand behind the home plate fence and judge for yourself. Looking back, it makes me realize how much simpler things were in those days. It was nothing short of amazing that so much talent could be assembled in that little town."

In the Merchants' early years, television barely existed in Durand. It was invented in the 1930s but was slow to become popular because a TV set was expensive. A five-inch, black-and-white RCA set housed in a large boxy wooden cabinet cost $350 in 1946, more than a month's salary for the average U.S. worker. About 40,000 sets were sold in 1946, the same year there were 40 million radios in America. But television started to take off in 1948, when three-inch sets sold for as little as $100. By the end of 1949, there were two million TV sets in the United States.

A year later there were eight million.

The Haggertys were the first Durand family to get a television set, probably in 1949. Bill's dad, Frank "Ted" Haggerty, won the set with a raffle ticket he purchased at a meeting of Chevrolet dealers in Chicago. He bought the winning ticket for 75 cents and it included the installation of the TV and an outside antenna. The donors had not counted on the winner living 90 miles from Chicago, which would require a large, expensive antenna. But they lived up to the deal and installed a huge tower outside Haggerty's house that was at least 60 feet tall. The direction of the antenna was controlled by a device that rested on top of the TV set. The closest TV stations were in Chicago and Davenport, Iowa. The set took two to four minutes to warm up and the picture was snowy a lot of the time. The reception from the Davenport station was somewhat better than from Chicago stations.

Joe Beurkle, who owned and lived above the cheese factory at the south edge of town, got Durand's second television set. That was a lucky break for me and my family because the Beurkles were members of our block rosary group, which met once a week to pray the rosary. That meant we visited the Beurkles at least once a month and always stayed afterward to watch professional boxing on the Gillette Friday Night Fights. The picture was often snowy but you could usually make out the fighters. The sound came and went. Clear reception didn't arrive until 1953 when Rockford's first television station — WTVO, an NBC affiliate — went on the air on May 3.

Until then, radio was king in everyone's homes. Our family would gather at night around the radio, which was housed in a large cabinet about 4 feet 6 inches tall, in the living room and listen to our favorite shows. Mine included Amos and Andy, Edgar Bergen and Charlie McCarthy, Fibber McGee and Molly, the Shadow, the Green Hornet, the Cisco Kid and Our Miss Brooks. When we lived in 1952 in the one room schoolhouse while my father was remodeling our house in town, I remember lying in bed listening late at night to the Rocky Marciano-Jersey Joe Walcott heavyweight boxing championship fight. Dad had strung up a series of blankets the length of the room, behind which were all of the beds. The radio in the living room on the other side of the blankets could be easily heard. Listening to Marciano, who was losing the fight, knock out Walcott in the 13th round is burned into my brain as if it happened yesterday. So are hundreds of Saturday night baths in the kitchen. Since we didn't have indoor plumbing at the schoolhouse or the house in town until its renovation was completed in 1953, our weekly baths consisted of sitting in a metal round tub as our mother poured water warmed on the stove over us.

For many of us, softball games were the highlight of the two-week school held each summer at St. Mary's Catholic Church to study the Baltimore Catechism. Nuns from Chicago, including Sister Euchrista, the sister of the parish priest, Father Joseph A. Driscoll, and Sister Nicolina taught the classes in the church basement. At recess each day, Father Driscoll, a big man at about 6 feet one-inch tall and weighing 220 pounds, would umpire standing behind the pitcher on the diamond in the lot west of the church rectory. Sometimes he would pitch. If a batter hit the ball in the garden in right field, a double was awarded — no outfielder was allowed to chase down a ball in the garden. Our secret desire was to hit a ball far enough in left field to break a window at the rectory. One day it happened. Father Driscoll was pitching to Bill Flynn, who smashed a ball over the heads of everyone in left field (each team sometimes had 13 or 14 players) and demolished a window in the rectory. We all told Father Driscoll we sure were sorry that happened, but we all were not-so-secretly delighted that Bill did the deed.

If we weren't entertaining ourselves by playing sports, we were playing games. Kick the Can was a favorite. Essentially, one player was "it" and set up a can at the home base. Everyone else had 30 seconds to hide somewhere on the designated playing ground. The player who was "it" then had to find and tag them. Once tagged, players returned to the home base and could be freed only if another player ran to home base and kicked the can before being tagged. The can then had to be returned to its original position and the tag game started again. We would play Kick the Can until it got dark and then would catch lightning bugs and put them in jars. At some point, usually about 9 p.m., everyone would break up and walk home — no parents ever chauffeured a child in a car, even at night.

Another favorite pastime was building and playing in a two-story tree house on the west side of our home on East Main Street. My brother Dave and I, Bill Haggerty and the Keller brothers, Donnie and Raymond, spent hours finding scraps of wood around town. Most of it came from the crates that held small machinery in the John Deere storage shed just west of our house or from scraps left over at Durand Plumbing & Heating, next to the Deere storage shed. It took us weeks to build the house about 25 feet off the ground in a large box elder tree between our house and the Deere shed. When we completed the job, kids from all over town took turns climbing the tree to see the house.

While the tree house was an impressive accomplishment, it paled in comparison to the Shack that Jim Spelman and Jim Walsh built in 1956 near the railroad tracks behind Walsh's house on West Howard Street. Even more impressive than the Shack was the fact that Spelman and Walsh slept in it nearly every night for four years, until they both went off to college and other schooling.

Jim Spelman tells better than anyone the tale of teen-agers pushing for independence and freedom:

> "When the Mulvain barn was torn down in the neighborhood, just three doors east of the Walsh home, and we were offered free lumber, the idea of a shack by the tracks was born. We pooled our money and bought some nails and roofing paper and borrowed a few boards from the sawmill on the other side of the tracks near Pete Robb's place. At age 14, neither of us knew anything about construction but somehow, with no power tools, we were able to cobble up this 10 x 15 foot shack with a shed roof and two small windows born from drawings on a piece of paper. With a smoke stack and a TV antenna sticking out of the roof, it looked like something right out of Southern Arkansas. And, to top it off, it was within 50 yards of the railroad tracks.

> "The tracks were the main line for the Milwaukee Road Railroad. Durand had six crossings in town but only one with lighted

signals. So the trains came through blasting their horns at every crossing. And with the shack so close to the tracks, it was LOUD.

"Allen Amundsen (grandfather of Mike Waller), who lived next door to the Walshes, provided a kerosene stove, a fuel tank to hang on the wall and an old recliner chair for our new home. We carried kerosene to the shack every other night throughout the winter months in a 5-gallon can that cost about a buck fifty to fill. We had absolutely no insulation and hung tar paper on the walls to cut down on the wind coming through the cracks. The extra breeze was probably all that kept us from getting asphyxiated. However, on nights where temperatures dropped to 20 below zero or more, the temperature inside our little abode would be about 68 to 70 degrees.

"We also had a couch, a chair and a roll-a-way cot with horizontal springs and a 4-inch mattress. The two of us couldn't fit in the shack without making contact, but you weren't going to have a square dance inside. We didn't care because we were out of the house and 'on our own.' We were too young to drive but constantly pushing the envelope for any kind of independence and freedom. Both of us always rode motorbikes without a license and drove cars, trucks and tractors since both our dads were in the farm tractor and implement business — one John Deere and one Ford. But that never created any rivalry between us or our families.

"We soon realized we needed electricity and, with the help of Amundsen, put up a few poles and strung together drop cords to reach from the light socket on the Walsh back porch to the shack. What a treat to have electric lights and a television. That started our parents 'watching us' to see what time the lights went out, signaling bed time. They warned us that if we didn't go to bed earlier than when we were home, we'd have to come back home. So, if 10:30 was the curfew, we'd turn out the lights, put an army blanket over the windows so it looked dark, turned the lights back on and went to bed when we felt like it. Other times, we told our parents we were going to the shack to retire for the evening. We'd turn on the light making them think we were inside, then head off to wherever we were going. They were never aware of what all went on.

"In the winter, the heat generated from the stove attracted field mice since we were in the middle of a field and one of them found its way into the TV set and built a nest. Soon the TV crapped out and a very strange odor appeared on the scene. I remember using a pencil to flick 10 baby mice out of the TV into a waste basket. I don't think Stan Panoske appreciated us bringing the TV out to his farm, expecting him to fix it. Of course, it was not fixable, so we had to bum another TV off of someone else for our viewing pleasure.

"There were never any drugs or alcohol involved with the shack. It was pretty much off limits to the girls, not that there were any dumb enough to want to go there. We had a few stag parties there that were a lot of fun. One afternoon Coach Sid Felder arranged for the high school basketball team to have the afternoon off to rest up for that night's regional tournament game against Belvidere. But most of the team spent the afternoon hanging out at the shack. The team won anyway, Durand's first victory ever in the state regional tournament.

"The Standing Rule was 'what goes on at the shack stays at the shack.' But everyone in town knew about the shack. It was unique.

"The shack generated a lot of stories. One of the funniest involved 'Wilson,' a John Deere salesman who came to Durand for an open house showing of new John Deere tractors. Wilson got totally smashed and became bound and determined he was going to spend the night with us at the shack. He came staggering in and crashed like a bull elephant. At about 3 a.m. one of those nightly trains made its normal route through town within the 50 yard distance of the shack. Wilson had sobered up just enough to hear it. But he had no idea where he was and immediately thought he must be in the middle of the railroad tracks, and was about to die. He got out of bed, turned on the overhead light, shocking us out of a deep sleep, and opened the door only to see the headlights of a train bearing down on him. I yelled for him to turn off the light. He yelled, 'Where am I?' and I replied that he would soon be on his way to heaven if he didn't turn off that light. We assured him he was not in the middle of railroad tracks and he would be all right. I doubt if he believed us until the train passed.

"There are many other stories like this. But…what goes on at the shack stays at the shack.

"After we grew out of the shack, it sat there vacant for a few years. Eventually it was torched, along with some cherished memories of a childhood that neither of us would want to trade for anything.

"To this day, it surprises both of us that our parents let us stay down there all that time. I certainly wouldn't allow any of my kids to do that, even if I knew nothing out-of-sorts was going on there."

Some of us also loved playing croquet. For a couple of years, Russ Sarver and I played more than 500 matches, keeping a running score for the summer. Playing cowboys and Indians, especially after watching a Western movie at the free show, and catching pollywogs down by the pond near the old grade school, were other favorite pastimes. So was collecting and trading baseball cards. We would do all sorts of jobs — mow lawns and cemeteries, set pins at the bowling alley for 10 cents a line, bale hay for $5 a day at area farms, wash cars for $1, shovel sidewalks in the winter — to earn enough money to buy the cards, a nickel for a pack of five and some awful-tasting bubble gum. By the time I was 17 years old, I had collected more than 7,000 baseball cards. Not knowing that someday they would be worth a fortune in mint condition, I pinned them on the walls of my bedroom with thumb tacks, played games with them and put them in bicycle spokes to create a motor bike sound. Alas, I wound up with barely a few cards in even good condition and no fortune.

We also spent a lot of time fishing and skinny dipping in the north and south branches of Otter Creek, less that a half-mile from town. The water was dirty, sometimes with sewage, but that didn't matter to us. A special treat was when Mike Mulvain and Jim Walsh would convince Gazette reporter "Buzz" Stauffer to drive some of us to Monroe, Wis., to go swimming in the city's public pool. Now and then Stauffer, an excellent diver, agreed and chauffeured us to the pool 20 miles north of Durand.

Stauffer wasn't our only chauffeur before we were old enough to drive. My dad drove me and my buddies Mo Ostergard and Bill Haggerty to a few Beloit College basketball games in the early 1950s. Beloit had great teams then, starring such players at Bob Donahue, Mack Stanley and John Brooks. Dolph Stanley was the coach and compiled a 238-57 won-loss record from 1945 to 1957.

For my 16th birthday, Dad took me and Bill Haggerty to a Braves-Reds baseball game in Milwaukee. Warren Spahn pitched well but was beaten 1-0 on a home run by Cincinnati's Ted Kluszewski. Afterward, we stopped at a restaurant where Bill and I told the hostess we were sons of Braves third baseman Eddie Mathews. We got seated quickly, though it's doubtful the hostess believed us.

Another chauffeur was a pilot, Roy Geist, husband of Gladys Geist, our first-grade teacher. Roy had massive arms and in his prime was considered one of the strongest men in the area, along with Howard Fosler and Lawrence "Humphrey" Brace, according to Mo Ostergard. Roy loved flying his single engine plane but didn't like flying alone, so he often took passengers with him. Once, in the fall of 1954, Roy invited Mo, who invited me, to Iowa City to see Iowa play a Big 10 football game. The main attraction was Iowa's great All-American offensive guard, Calvin Jones.

A couple of years later, most of my buddies owned their own cars. They loved working on them as much as driving them.

They and a lot of older guys loved racing around town square park and using Center Street Road north of town as a drag strip. Since there were no town police they were rarely in any jeopardy of being arrested.

Glass pack mufflers were the rage at the time. They wouldn't work on Mo's '54 Chevy flathead 6 cylinder engine; a V-8 engine was required to generate all the noise. A lot of guys got the mufflers installed at Warshawskys at the corner of South Main and Cedar Street in Rockford (it is still in business there today).

As the mufflers aged, they became louder. Few were louder than those on Doug Sweet's family car — you could hear them from the high school to the Mile Corner south of town.

One day in the spring of 1960, Doug and Mo were walking out of Jim Slocum's Gulf service station on the east end of town square park, headed to their parked cars. Suddenly, two guys in an unmarked police car pulled up behind Doug's car and wouldn't let him back out. They hopped out of their car, and Mo immediately recognized them as Rockford police detectives. They walked up to Doug and one of them said, "We have a complaint from a local citizen about your loud car. I don't want to hear about that again."

He then took out his gloves and slapped Doug across the face with them. "That's nothing," he told Doug. "I'll really rough you up if I'm called out to Durand again because of your loud mufflers."

Mo froze in fear.

"I thought I was going to be next, simply by being with Doug," he said. "But they left me alone."

You never heard Doug show off his loud glass packs after that.

A lot of Durand teen-agers, including Tom Spelman, loved driving their cars out to Doc Waller's farm near the Wisconsin state line and race down the steep hills, especially with snow on the ground in the winter. Big crowds gathered to watch drivers roll their cars. Miraculously, no one was ever hurt. When Tom's dad Leo, who owned the Ford tractor dealership and the DX Service Station, found out about Tom's daredevil ways, he sent one of his employees with a sledgehammer to smash the engine of Tom's 1948 Ford.

Tom loved auto racing and one year he, Mike Mulvain and Bill

Parsons drove from Durand to the Daytona 500 race. Tom was sleeping in the back seat and Mike was driving as they crossed into Florida in the early morning hours. Tom woke up and lit up a cigarette with his flame-controlled lighter. The flame shot too high and set his hair on fire. He flailed away putting out the blaze in his dark wavy hair as Mike and Bill shook with laughter.

But perhaps the most fun we had came when we played at what Mike Mulvain and my cousin Don Waller called "the most exciting corner in town." It probably should have been called the Forbidden Zone, because that's what our parents thought it should be. It was located on the corner of Oak and Water streets, about 100 yards from our back door and at the corner where Don lived. The attractions there were luring and off-limits. Across Water Street from Don's house was the town water tower, which was built in 1928 and was at least 200 feet tall. It had crisscross iron bars every foot or so that you could use for steps but no one was supposed to climb on them. But we all did. Most of us got no higher than the first railing, about one-third of the way up to the top. Don and Mike climbed to the second railing many times.

"But most of us never got past the second railing, it was just too high," Don recalled. "There is a walkway with a railing at the bottom of the tank at the top of the tower. A ladder leads from the walkway to the top of the tank. Another ladder lays on the roof of the tank that goes to the ball on the very top. The only person I know who climbed all the way to the top was Pete Adleman, who was the water commissioner. My brother Ken made it up the walkway ladder and used to throw homemade parachutes tied to fishing sinkers over the railing. There was a cable hanging from the top with a float in the water to measure how much was in the tower. The wind would blow and the cable would clang against the side of the tower. A large pipe running from the ground to the bottom of the tank burst one winter. It made a loud noise and water came rushing out of the seams. Before long, we had ice all over the street around our house that didn't melt for weeks."

Pete Adleman wasn't the only climber to make it to the top of the water tower. My nephew, Dave Waller Jr., did it several times and so did Dan Highland (son of Merchant first baseman Dick Highland) and some of his buddies, including Jim Larson.

Next to the water tower was the Wertheimer Cattle Company stockyards that housed cattle, sheep and some horses. "Whitey" Astrup was the manager and didn't mind if kids hung around. We often raced on the six-inch wooden rail on top of the fences surrounding the stockyards, pretending we were acrobats. "We would get a bucket of oats from Graham's elevator up the street and take it to the stockyards," said Don Waller. "We'd then coax a horse to come to the fence to eat the oats and jump on his back and ride him. We'd go home smelling like horses and catch cane from my mother. One Halloween my brother Ken and I swiped the stockyard's wooden manure spreader and pulled it over to the vault factory. Then we'd laugh and laugh as we watched folks try to pull it back to the stockyards."

The vault factory — the Charles Miller Company, which manufactured burial vaults — was another hot spot at the hub. It was just around the corner on the north side of Oak Street. "Charlie Miller never locked up the place," Don Waller said. "We'd take our BB guns and play with them over there until one night I accidentally shot my cousin Bob Rice between the eyes. After that we left the BB guns at home." Years later, after Don had died, his brother Ken acknowledged at a service for Don that it was him, not Don, who had shot Bob Rice.

A BB gun got me in plenty of hot water, too. We used to make wooden guns with clothes line pins that could shoot rubber bands and have fights between East End and West End kids. My parents forbid any of us from having BB guns but one day I somehow got possession of one. In a skirmish one afternoon at the Dickerson home on West Main Street I fired a shot into the open barn loft behind their house and struck one of the five Dickerson brothers, Mark, in the eye. My father was called and I was hauled back home, where I feared a beating awaited. Instead, my dad told me to sit in a chair on the front lawn until the state police came to take me to jail. I sat there from dawn to dusk for three straight days before I figured out the state police were never coming.

The state highway garage on the west side of Don Waller's house was another favorite place on "the most exciting corner." Behind it was a huge pile of cinders, dumped on icy roads in winter to help make them passable. It was off limits but too big a temptation for most of us to pass up. Just a few minutes romping around the pile left you black and sooty and often led to a severe spanking.

Another fun spot near the corner, and not forbidden, was Bud Haughton's Auto Body Shop, a building or two west of the state highway garage. Haughton was involved in stock car racing and it was a treat to visit his shop and listen to him rev up the engine and tell stories about racing.

The last place near "the most exciting corner" that was a site of many thrills was the railroad depot and its tracks. For years the Chicago, Milwaukee and St. Paul Railroad Company operated several freight and passenger trains each day, mainly because Durand — unlike most small towns — could accommodate them with its three switch tracks. The trains carried commodities such as coal, cattle and the U.S. mail. Darting between the tracks as trains were waiting to be switched was great fun, though dangerous.

Not all our activity was in the Forbidden Zone. One of my favorite spots was Slocum's Gulf service station. Actually, it was the south brick wall of the Yale Building next to the station. I spent hours there nearly every Sunday afternoon when the station was closed throwing rubber baseballs at the wall, fielding the returning ground balls and pitching to a chalk target on the wall.

That little corner was often bustling with some kind of activity. Doctors Young and Frame had their dentists' offices on the second floor of the Yale Building, where Doctor Schwartz had one too.

Mike Mulvain recalls harrowing visits to the dentist. First came the walk up the long, steep flight of stairs to the second floor.

Then came the business of the day — the dentist's chair. "No Novocaine or any other pain killer was used, so getting a tooth pulled was a traumatic experience," Mike recalled. "That's how Doc Young got his nickname — Yank-'Em Young."

My brother Dave can attest to the pain at the top of the stairs. In the mid- or late 1940s he was bitten in the mouth by a mixed mutt owned by Maurice Corwin. Dave said it was his fault, not the dog's, because Dave accidently stepped on its foot.

Dave was rushed to Dr. Schwartz's second floor office. Jim Slocum, Ted Augustine and a couple of other service station patrons were quickly recruited to hold down Dave as the doctor stitched up the wound — without a pain killer.

Another favorite spot for me and my three brothers and sister was our uncle's cabin off Judd Road a few miles south of town. Marsden Place, June Amundsen and Rod Doty built a cabin there alongside the Pecatonica River in 1944. It had one large room, about 25 feet by 35 feet, and a screened-in porch that could sleep 6 people on matresses.

For years Marsden, a Rockford fireman, held regular poker games there with his firemen buddies. Now and then he would invite our family to visit the cabin, where I often played Cowboy and Indians with my cousin Jim Place. It was a rugged terrain, forcing Marsden and June to build a swinging bridge over a creek to get to the cabin.

A fresh-water spring was nearby, and rain water was collected off the roof in a 55-gallon barrel to wash the dishes. On the east side of the cabin car batteries were hooked up to a generator to supply electricity. Inside, the large room had a large table, some chairs, a couch that doubled as a bed, a cupboard for the dishes and a gun cabinet. Less from 50 yards from the porch was the river, a good 20 steps down a steep bank to the water. Fishing and hunting on the river bank were popular pursuits.

It felt like the Wild West.

It wasn't the only cabin in our lives.

Bliss's cabin, on East South Street in Durand across from Louie Thomas's home and a couple of stone throws from the high school, was the site of many parties after school events such as football and basketball games or the junior and senior proms. Denny Bliss, my classmate, hosted much late-night imbibing there. It was a safe haven for treating yourself to some adult beverages.

Drinking to excess caused a few issues. Once a cap somehow ended up covering the chimney, forcing the smoke from the fireplace back down into the room. Denny lept into action, climbed up on the roof and removed the cap. Unfazed by the incident, everyone walked across the street and woke up Louis Thomas, whose wife served breakfast while everyone waited for the smoke to clear.

One year after the junior class prom, Bill Haggerty joined Denny and several other visitors at the cabin. But first Bill drove home the family car and parked it in the garage, then walked back down to the cabin to join in the merry-making. Hours later he managed to get home and into bed.

When his parents got up the next morning, they noticed the car was missing in front of the house on West Main, where it usually was parked. No one thought to look in the garage. They panicked and began calling around to find Bill. When they had no luck, Bill's dad, Ted Haggerty, drove around town looking for Bill. Still no luck. At about 11 a.m., Bill's mother, Bernice, checked upstairs in his bedroom. There was Bill, still trying to sleep off a tough night.

But all the searching alerted many folks around town, including Coach Sid Felder, that Bill had been missing after a night at Bliss's cabin. It proved to be a costly evening for Bill. Coach Felder dismissed him from the track team for violating team rules. It was a big loss for Bill and the team because Bill was a star sprinter. Years later Bill said Felder had no choice but to suspend him.

Bill was just one of several athletes that Felder kept on a straight and narrow path. In the fall of 1957, a year and a half after Mike's dad Lloyd Mulvain was killed in a power line accident near Shirland, Mike was having a difficult time adjusting. He was a sophomore playing on the freshman-sophomore basketball team but had become rebellious, staying out late at night and engaging in after-hours mischief. Mike wasn't getting along with Coach Milt Truesdale and finally announced he was quitting the team.

Felder, a good friend of Lloyd's, quickly heard of Mike's decision. He chased Mike down on the steps of the old high school, grabbed him by the collar, told him he couldn't quit and henceforth would be a member of the varsity team, where Felder could keep an eye on him.

"It changed my life," Mike remembered. "I was out of control and Felder and sports kept me in school."

Other activity was less exciting than basketball shenanigans or Bliss's cabin.

My three brothers and sister and I spent many hours each summer working in our gardens and harvesting the vegetables. We had a garden about 10 feet by 40 feet in our back yard and another, much larger one across from our house on East Main Street not far from the Methodist Church. We spent many afternoons and evenings snipping green beans and podding green peas, a boring chore. My mother canned well over 100 quarts each year of tomatoes, green beans, peas and other vegetables. We also grew a lot of potatoes. Our family ate about 100 pounds every two weeks.

Each spring we made several trips to area forests to hunt for morels, an edible mushroom. Soaked in salt water to chase away the bugs and fried in egg batter and cracker crumbs, morels were delicious, so rich that you could eat only a few of them at a sitting. They often were found on the forest floor around dead trees and popped up out of the ground fully grown. We usually found some, but sometimes came home empty-handed. But when Roy Wilke accompanied us, we always came home with plenty of mushrooms. As a timber man, he was a genius at spotting them. Often when he returned from timber-buying trips, he stopped by our house with a sackful of mushrooms.

One of our favorite hangouts was the Durand Cafe, on the west side of town square park. It was owned by Carl Nuss, who kept the official scorebook or umpired at many Merchant games, and his wife Winnie. They made great cherry Cokes and hamburgers and had the only juke box in town. It was a fun place but so was the spot next door, Bill Steward's barbershop. Mo Ostergard, another baseball buddy and a terrific pitcher, remembered it fondly:

> "Bill's barbershop was a home away from home for young boys. It was also a library. He had the Police Gazette, Life Magazine, the Saturday Evening Post and the Sporting News, the major

league's baseball Bible. He hated the New York Yankees. Russ Sarver, Lawrence Damon and I were big Yankee fans and Bill was unmerciful to us in attacking the Yankees. I sometimes thought he would cut off my ears just to get a point across. No one could cut a flat top like Bill. That was the big haircut in the '50s. Once my brother Harv came home from Bill's with a Mohawk haircut and my mother just about died. I thought she was going to walk into his shop with a butcher knife, but it wasn't Bill's fault. Harv quickly convinced her that the Mohawk was his idea. He was the talk of the town for weeks. I always remembered Bill watching us play Little League and Pony League baseball. I was the pitcher for most of those games and at times it wasn't pretty. Bill would always come up after a bad game and say, 'Mo, don't worry about it. You'll get them next time.' That always meant a lot to me."

In his early years, Mo was an outstanding pitcher. He won many games with his humming fastball in Little League and Pony League games. In eighth grade Mo pitched both ends of a double-header — 14 innings in all — and won both games at Roscoe. But by the time he entered high school, his arm was shot. At that time, there were no rules governing how many innings a player could pitch a week. Firing his fastball often and throwing curves at an early age ruined his pitching career.

The Merchants also were a big part of the lives of the Dickerson brothers. There are five of them — Steve, John, Jim, Mark and Greg — and all were outstanding students. The family moved from Rockford to Durand in 1946. The Dickersons lived in Laona Township near Durand from about 1840 to 1900. With the move back to Durand, the sons became the sixth consecutive generation living in the town. The oldest, Steve, recalled fondly his boyhood in Durand:

> "The Merchants' games were a favorite evening spectator event. I remember collecting Popsicle sticks at the games. If you collected enough, you could redeem them for prizes. The prize I most remembered was a fixed blade knife about six inches long.
>
> "My first day in first grade included meeting Jane Walsh, who

wondered why all my worksheets from Garrison Grade School in Rockford had the letter E (for Excellent) instead of an A. I was called on to read that day. I stood up and read, causing a stir. In Durand, one did not stand up.

"The walk to the old grade school was seven blocks and we went home for lunch. That first winter introduced me to long walks in the snow, dogs that were threatening, and tadpoles and pussy willows in the pond next to the railroad track that was crossed on the way to school. One day in the second grade I started crying because the class had not been dismissed for lunch on time. When asked why I was crying, I told the teacher, Gladys Geist, that the delay was going to cause me to miss lunch. She pointed out that I had misread the clock at the front of the room.

"Recess often involved a game of softball. I was usually picked pretty late in the process. What I remember most about recess was me finally cleaning the clock of the class bully and Jerry Cooper repeating his favorite expression: 'As thin as a mosquito's ass stretched across a barrel.'

"Beginning in the fourth grade, I was the class president and Jane was usually the secretary. We were good friends and by the third grade I had picked her out as the one I wanted to marry. But we didn't date until the Halloween dance in our junior year, where we arrived separately but left as high-school sweethearts. Jane and I have now been married for 45 years.

"We had exceptional parents who gave us great opportunities. Dad organized a troop of the Cub Scouts so that we could participate. He took John and me on train trips to Chicago when he had business meetings. At one time Dad and Mom were joint president of the PTA (parent-teachers' association). Dad provided us with a gas engine — a washing machine motor — and a variable speed belt drive apparatus so that we could build the first go-cart in town in about sixth grade (1953). He also got us a 1939 Hudson that we took apart in about eighth grade so that we could understand cars. We also got a 1946 Crosley that we made into a Masaratti-like vehicle with a hand-made fiberglass body, a new frame and very low seats. And we had the one and only trampoline in town, which attracted other kids to the house.

"Beginning in seventh grade, we started being concerned about raising money for our senior trip. I remember growing cucumbers for sale to a pickle processing plant to raise funds. In the cucumber business, it is very desirable to pick them when they are small because that gets a higher price. But we couldn't keep up with our one-acre field between Howard Street and the railroad tracks, so although we had a good deal of tonnage we produced very little revenue."

Steve and his younger brother John, who was my classmate in the 1940s and 1950s, were both good athletes. Steve excelled at track and field and for some time held the school record for the 100 and 220-yard dashes. John was a key player on the school basketball, baseball and football teams. John, like Steve, remembered his days in Durand as special:

"Our home was across the street from the Methodist parsonage on West Main Street, so we joined the Methodist Church. My Dad tithed religiously but never went to church — he already knew the word of God. Not so with me. I was in church every Sunday. The rest of my time was consumed with sports, music, girls and education.

"My first grade teacher, Mrs. Geist, taught me how to speak and write notes to girls. Pat Adleman made eyes at me on the first day of school and was my sweetheart until the fourth grade when Jim Cowen moved to Durand. He later moved to Rockford and starred on the East High School basketball team. Bill "Cork Butt" Haggerty was the first person in town with a TV and he became my best friend. Sue Waller (my cousin) was my next love, but

Larry Damon outscored me in every basketball game and I lost Sue within a year. I then turned to playing clarinet, knowing that Cowen and Damon had no musical talents.

"Rubber-band guns were introduced into Durand after a visit Steve and I had with DeWitt Main after he moved to Mount Carroll and learned the art.

"My seventh grade teacher, Helen Johnson, encouraged me to join the basketball team since I was the tallest boy in the class. It was fortunate that the coaches, Mr. Truesdale and Mr. Felder, were my neighbors. I played on the first team, without distinction, until graduation. I was left-handed so I played first base and pitcher on the baseball team. The last game I pitched I loaded the bases, so the coach suggested I take a full windup. I did, and the guy on third stole home during my windup. The other team started laughing. It wasn't that funny to me. To this day, the Durand Bulldog banner hangs in my room and with it the memories of my teammates Cowen, Damon, Haggerty and Waller.

"Oh, did I mention, in my junior year after a game with Pecatonica in which I grabbed 10 rebounds and scored 10 points — a double double — that Alice Walsh smiled at me? She was impressed that on top of the double double I also played in the band at halftime. We sat next to each other at the dance after the game and held hands. Alice broke my heart two years later.

"Let me leave you with one final remark: Only in Durand could you grow up and have so many opportunities to learn, love and participate, and even lose. I wish everyone could be so lucky."

Charles "Buzz" Stauffer, left, and Lionel "Curley" Weaver, right, enjoy a beer. Stauffer sometimes would drive some of us youngsters 20 miles north of Durand to Monroe, Wis., to swim in the city's public pool.

The Durand Cheese Factory in the 1950s at the corner of East South and Center streets facing Route 70. It was owned by Joe Buerkle and his son, Joe Jr. The Buerkles lived in an apartment above the factory and owned the second television set in Durand. Frank "Ted" Haggerty owned the first one, won with a 75-cent raffle ticket at a Chevrolet dealers' meeting in 1949. (Photo courtesy of Kevin Steward).

Durand's United Methodist Church, at the north end of the town square park. (Photo courtesy of Helen C. Johnson).

The house on East Main Street in which I grew up, as it looked in June 2007. Gone were the front porch and the box elder tree on the right side of the house where we built a two-story tree house. (Photo by Mike Waller).

The Durand Barber Shop, left, and the Masonic Temple, on the west side of town square park, as they looked in June 2007. They look the same as they did in the 1950s. The barber shop was owned and operated for more than 30 years by Bill "The Barber" Steward. (Photo by Mike Waller).

St. Mary's Catholic Church, on West Main Street, in the 1970s. The rectory is at the right and on the other side of it was the diamond where we played softball at recess from catechism classes during summer school. (Photo courtesy of Mo Ostergard and Dennis Bliss).

The Durand water tower, in a photo taken by me in June 2007 from the alley behind our house on East Main Street. It looked much the same in the 1950s, when we would climb it. I never got higher than the first railing. It was torn down on June 20, 2009 and replaced at another location.

Jim Spelman, left, and Jim Walsh years after they lived as teen-agers in the Shack.

The Shack, down by the railroad tracks behind Jim Walsh's home. (Photo by Jim Spelman).

From left, Jim Place, Mike Mulvain and Mike Waller visit Marsden Place's cabin along the Pecatonica River in 2014. (Photo by Dave Waller).

From left, Donald Flynn, Jim Slocum, Ted Haggerty, Dr. Victor Frame and Leo Spelman. All were Durand cheerleaders and Flynn and Haggerty were members of the first board of directors at The Durand State Bank.

From left, Russ Sarver and Dave Waller, front row, and Mike Waller and Mo Ostergard, back row, playing baseball in Sarver's front yard on West Main Street in the early 1950s.

Mike Waller, left, and Mike Mulvain with Mulvain's Mercury at Louie Thomas' service station a mile south of Durand in the late 1950s.

130 DURAND'S MARVELOUS MERCHANTS

CHAPTER 7

Wilke's Swan Song

The Merchants' opening game for 1953 was still six weeks off when Gazette reporter Charles A. "Buzz" Stauffer made some news of his own. Running unopposed in the town elections in April, Stauffer was elected village clerk with 132 votes, an impressive total in a town of about 600 people. The mayor, Ernie Baker, was re-elected even though his name did not appear on the ballot. His friends rallied to his support with a write-in campaign.

Village clerk-reporter Stauffer was on hand Sunday night, June 7, when the Merchants opened the 1953 season at Legion Field in front of a "large and enthusiastic crowd" with a lineup that was missing two of their star hitters, third baseman Wayne Adleman and shortstop Lloyd Mulvain. Adleman was playing that year for his employer's team, Rockford's Woodward Governor, and player-manager Mulvain kept himself out of the lineup.

But it didn't matter. Durand scored six runs in the fourth inning to overcome a 5-1 deficit and defeat Barber-Coleman of Rockford 8-7. Roy Wilke pitched the first four innings, giving up four hits and five runs. Jack Sharp tossed the last three innings and gave up only two singles. Sharp and second baseman Johnny Hartman led the Merchants with two hits each. Wilke, catcher Jerry Mulvain, first baseman Vernal Jones and left fielder Fred Geiser chipped in with one hit each, according to the partial box score that was back in the Gazette after being dropped in mid-season a year earlier.

Wilke was in better form the following Wednesday. He scattered four hits and got spectacular support in the field as the Merchants defeated a very good Juda, Wis., team 4-1. Hartman, Geiser and center fielder Joe Hines all turned in sparkling catches. Sharp gave Wilke all the runs he needed with a two-run home run.

Two nights later, the Merchants ran their winning streak to three on the strength of Johnnie Smith's six-hit pitching and 10 hits by his teammates. Durand scored eight runs in the second inning and defeated Rockford's Globe Imperial 11-6. Jerry Mulvain and Hines each had a double and a single and Hartman had two singles.

Wilke was back on the mound Sunday night, June 14, and had a no-hitter for five and two-thirds innings. He wound up with a two-hitter and 12 strikeouts as the Merchants beat Rockford's Woodward Governor 5-3. Nine walks kept Wilke in trouble most of the night. Woodward Governor threatened in the top of the seventh inning when Wilke gave up a single and two walks with one out. But he got out of the jam by striking out former Merchant star Adleman and getting a ground ball to first base for the final out. Jack McMahon, playing third base, led Durand with two runs scored and one hit.

The Merchants' unbeaten string soared to five as they won a tense 2-1 thriller on Friday night, June 26, over Rockford's Marine Reserve team. Wilke pitched a three-hitter while striking out 13 and walking only three. Both teams struck in the opening inning. The Marines scored a run as they got two of their three hits with only one out. But Wilke shut them down by striking out the next two batters. The Merchants got their two runs in the bottom of the first on a walk to Jones, a triple by Bernie Figi, who was playing second base, and a passed ball. It was all Wilke needed. Lloyd Mulvain was hitless in his first game of the season.

The Merchants continued their winning ways on July 1 by easily defeating Rockford Atwoods 8-1 for their seventh victory in a row — the Gazette did not publish anything about their sixth win. Durand rapped out 11 hits as Wilke pitched a two hitter, striking out nine. Jerry Mulvain paced the Merchants' hit parade with a perfect three for three and scored two runs. Figi, playing third base, also had three hits. The game story announced that the Merchants would be host in early August to a 16-team invitational tournament at Legion Field. Teams from Iowa, Wisconsin and Illinois were invited and the winner would take home $200.

The Gazette also reported on the winners of various competitions at Durand's annual July 4th celebration. First prize for best boys' bicycle went to Jim Walsh, with second place going to Ron Adleman. Shirley Adleman won first prize for best girls' bicycle. My dad, Ward Waller, won for having the largest family (seven) in attendance. Merchants Don Hubbartt and Lloyd Mulvain won the egg-throwing contest. Dick Cuthbertson gobbled his way to victory in the melon-eating contest. In the amateur talent contest, Linda Engebretson took first place, a Rockford boy won second place and I won third place singing my version of "Gone Fishing."

Other news in the Gazette included a story under the headline "HAS NARROW ESCAPE" about 11-year-old Dick Flynn, son of Donald and Virginia Flynn. Young Flynn fell from the back of a moving truck when the endgate became loose and pushed him off. "He received no broken bones but was badly bruised and lost a large part of the skin from his back and both elbows and has a 'bump' on his head," the story said.

But the biggest news with the biggest headline on the front page — "Believes Modern Youth Trustworthy" — was this report:

> "Charlie Traum found an honest man (boy) last week without the aid of Diogenes lantern.
>
> "Mr. Traum lost $52 in bills on Center Street in Durand last Wednesday. As soon as the loss was advertised in the Durand Gazette, Gary Tracy, 11-year-old son of the Chas. Tracys (the former manager of the Merchants), who had found the roll of bills, restored them to the owner.
>
> "This story should receive wide publicity to help refute some of the unfavorable stories about modern youth."

The Merchants, off to their best start ever, lost their first game of the season and ended their seven-game winning streak, on Wednesday, July 8, as one of Freeport's best teams, Knodle Brothers, defeated them 8-5 at Legion Field. Durand pitcher Johnnie Smith appeared sharp for the first four innings but tired in the fifth and sixth innings, giving up six runs. The Merchants were held to only five hits.

But Durand and Smith rebounded two nights later against Rockford Ordnance. The Merchants fell behind 6-0 in the first two innings as pitcher "Red" Barron had trouble getting anyone out. Smith relieved him and pitched one-hit ball in the last five innings. Durand could only muster one run and three hits in the first five innings. But the Merchants exploded in the sixth inning with five hits, four walks, three hit batsmen and 10 runs and won the game 11-7. Rookie third baseman Ken Ditzler played his first game of the season but was hitless. Hartman, Hines and Geiser each had two hits, according to the box score, the last one to appear in the Gazette not only for the season but for the rest of the Merchants games in their heyday. The most likely reason the paper quit publishing partial box scores was to save space. Reporter Stauffer and owner John R. Van Sickle had a long-standing dispute about how much coverage was adequate for the Merchants. Van Sickle wanted more space devoted to community news and less to softball. In the end, he would win the argument and lose the reporter.

The game story wound up with some bad news. Stauffer explained it:

> "A severe loss to the Merchant corps was announced the past week. Roy Wilke, a veteran star and owner of six straight wins this season, has taken a position with Curry-Miller Veneers, Inc., Indianapolis, Ind., and will be available to the team only on occasional weekends. Roy has rented most of his local logging equipment and is now traveling for the Indianapolis firm as a buyer specializing in walnut lumber."

But Wilke pitched the next three games. On Wednesday, July 15, Wilke, Smith and Barron all were ineffective and wild as Winnebago dealt the Merchants one of their worst defeats, 18-5. Pitcher Russ Stringer kept the Merchants in check as Winnebago scored 10 runs in the fourth inning and seven more in the fifth on 14 walks by Durand pitchers.

Wilke, with an assist from Geiser, won his seventh game in eight starts two nights later as the Merchants came from a 4-1 deficit in the sixth inning to edge Rockford Ni-Lint Tool 5-4. The game was tied 1-1 after five innings with Wilke and Ni-Lint's pitcher locked in a duel. But the Rockford team bunched three of its five hits in the sixth inning and took a comfortable 4-1 lead. Durand tied the game in the bottom of the sixth on singles by Hines and right fielder Bud Smith, an error and a double by Wilke. Geiser won the game for the Merchants in the bottom of the seventh with a two-out line drive single to center field that scored Hines from third.

Five years after Legion Field had been built, fans still flocked there by the hundreds to cheer on the Merchants. Jerry Mulvain's young daughters, Vicki and Linda, were on their best behavior at every game sitting on the laps of John and Helen Walsh, who rarely missed a game. Bernie Figi's young son was not easy to keep in tow. He didn't like walking barefooted so his mother removed his shoes to keep him sitting on the bleachers. The concession stand was enlarged and a few more bleachers were added. But otherwise, Legion Field looked much the same as it did when it was built.

The Merchants boosted their record to 10-2 on Sunday night, July 19, as they beat the Rockford Independents 4-2 before one of the largest crowds of the year at Legion Field. Wilke gave up only two hits as "11 Independents went down on strikeouts, with most of them swinging futilely under Wilke's deceptive 'upshoot.'" Durand hitters were led by a triple by Barron and doubles by Wilke and Figi.

Durand chalked up two more wins that week. The Merchants beat Rockford's B&K Tap 16-12 with a six-run outburst in the sixth inning. Geiser's triple and Gerald "Grub" McKearn's bases-loaded single were the big blows. The game story was one paragraph and offered no other details. It was the Gazette's only mention of McKearn, who was filling in for an absent regular.

Third baseman Adleman, missing playing with his Durand teammates, was back on the Merchants' roster for the first time in 1953 and led them to a 9-7 victory over Rockford National Lock on Friday, July 24. Adleman blasted the game-winning two-run home run in the bottom of the sixth inning after hitting a double and a single earlier. Wilke pitched a seven-hitter and struck out five to run the Merchants' season record to 12-2. It was the 10th win of the season without any losses against Rockford teams.

The Merchants suffered a jolt when the American Legion was forced to postpone the 16-team Durand Invitational Softball Tournament, which was scheduled to start in a week. The Gazette reported that failure of teams to enroll before the deadline was the chief cause of the postponement. But the paper said interest in the tournament continued and the Legion was planning to hold it later in August.

Another jolt came a week later in the form of the all-Negro Esquires team from Rockford. The outstanding Esquires, "a team of classy fielders and hitters," dealt Durand its third loss of the season, 7-5. Wilke gave up seven runs in the first four innings, including a three-run home run by the Esquires' third baseman. He then pitched hitless ball the rest of the game as his record fell to 9-2 for the season. Playing an all-Negro team in the early 1950s, before the Supreme Court ruled unconstitutional in 1954 the existence of segregated schools in America, was unusual but caused little stir among Durand fans.

July ended with the Gazette reporting on the appointment of a new minister for the Methodist Church. Earlier in the month, the church had honored the Rev. John J. Main and his family at a farewell party. The Rev. Mr. Main was appointed pastor of the Mt. Carroll Methodist Church. He was being replaced by the Rev. Samuel Weisshaar, who had been a pastor for 34 years in churches in Chicago, Baraboo, Wis., Forrest Park, Kirkland, McKinley Park and Popular Grove.

The Merchants lost their second straight game on Wednesday, Aug. 5, when Rockford Machine Tool blanked them, 6-0. It was the first time Durand had been shut out since August 1950 when Rockford's Parker Sporting Goods beat the Merchants 10-0. Machine Tool won the game in the first inning when Johnnie Smith gave up five hits and three runs. Rockford's "cocky but effective right-hander Carlson" had only one strikeout but retired 12 straight Durand hitters from the third to the seventh inning. Adleman's triple and Geiser's double were the Merchants' only hits.

Durand's hitting slump ended two nights later when the Merchants blasted 17 hits, seven for extra bases, in a 17-6 victory over American Cabinet of Rockford. Adleman led the parade with four hits, including a home run and two doubles. Smith, dubbed by reporter Stauffer as "Big Jawn" because of his 6-foot 3-inch and more than 200-pound physique, coasted in on an eight-hitter, striking out five and walking three.

The Merchants boosted their season record to 14-4 on Sunday

night, Aug. 9, when they defeated a team of free-lance players from Rockford's Industrial League 9-5. Bernie Figi, "the Merchants' all-around handyman," took a turn at pitching and came through with a solid four-hitter. Adleman once again led Durand's offense with two hits. Geiser also chipped in with two hits.

For the next five days, Durand fans were anxiously awaiting the rematch between the Merchants and Rockford Machine Tool. The wait was worth it. Friday night's game was "a tense, tight thriller that kept local fans squirming until the final out." Unfortunately, Machine Tool and its pitcher Carlson won again, this time 6-5 on a bases-loaded single in the seventh inning that broke a 5-5 tie. Machine Tool took a 2-0 lead in the first inning without Wilke giving up a hit, then scored three more runs in the fifth. Durand responded with four runs in the bottom of the fifth, though the Gazette story offered no details. The Merchants tied the game in the bottom of the sixth without the benefit of a hit on walks to third baseman Ken Ditzler and Smith and a pair of infield outs. But Wilke gave up a walk and three singles in the seventh inning that produced the winning run for Machine Tool.

It was a different story two nights later, on Sunday, Aug. 16. Wilke was steady on the mound and paced the Merchants' hitters with a home run, triple and double in leading Durand to a 13-3 victory over Rockford's Mechanics. Figi and Barron contributed two hits each. Stauffer then took the opportunity to praise the play of Ditzler:

> "One of the brightest spots in the locals' recent victories has been the terrific fielding play of rookie Kenny Ditzler. The youngster, playing his first season with the Merchants, has amazed veteran observers with his flawless play in the infield. Equally adept at second, short or third, Ditzler promises to be one of the smoothest performers in Durand's fine array of fielding talent."

The Merchants posted their 16th win of the season against five losses on Friday, Aug. 21, by defeating Rockford's Woodward Governor 5-3 for the second time in two months. Wilke pitched a five-hitter while striking out seven and walking three. Despite being held hitless for five innings, Durand took a 3-0 lead in the first inning on a bunch of walks and errors. The Merchants sealed the game in the sixth inning on a lead-off double by Hines and singles by Figi and Vernal Jones.

Most of the fans were looking ahead with excitement to Sunday night when the Merchants were scheduled to face the great James Vernon "Bullet" Kirk and Freeport's Knoodle Brothers, who had defeated Durand 8-5 six weeks earlier. But Johnnie Smith was pitching for the Merchants then. This time it would be Wilke on the mound. It was a game, Stauffer wrote, that few fans would forget:

> "Fresh from an appearance in Beloit's annual softball tournament in which he was beaten 1-0 after tossing nine innings of no-hit ball, Kirk flashed 18 strikeouts and doled only one hit as Freeport's Knoodle Brothers edged the Merchants, 2-1, at Legion Memorial Field.
>
> "Despite his amazing performance, Kirk needed — and got — a big break to defeat Durand's own brilliant chucker, Roy Wilke, who allowed only four hits and might easily have come off with a 1-0 win.
>
> "With one away in the fourth, and the score knotted at 0-0, Freeport's first baseman Currier drove a long double to right center field. Sorn then lashed a drive to short left field, and that was where the 'break' came.
>
> "In the absence of regular fielders Geiser and Barron, the Merchants had recruited Jack Yaun to patrol the left side of the garden. In making a desperate try for Sorn's liner, Yaun (who was not wearing spikes) lost his footing on the slippery outfield turf, and the ball went through for a triple, with Currier scoring. Sorn kept right on coming around third and scored when the relay from the infield went high and wild.
>
> "Wilke gave up only two other hits, both singles, but Kirk, who registered 13 straight strikeouts from the first to the sixth inning, kept right on breezing until the seventh when the Merchants got their run.
>
> "Lloyd Mulvain, pinch-hitting for Jones, drew a base on balls.

Adleman and Hartman both went down on strikes but Kirk then lapsed into a wild spell and hit both Smith and Ditzler to load the bases. With Barron at bat, the Freeport fireballer uncorked a wild pitch and Mulvain scored. With the winning runs on base, however, Kirk bore down with his uncanny speed and got Big Red on strikes to end the game.

"Durand's lone hit off Kirk came in the first inning. With one out, Joe Hines dropped a perfect bunt down the first base line. Neither the pitcher nor the first baseman could make a play on the ball.

"It marked Knodle's second win of the season over the Merchants and ran the locals' season mark to 16 wins and 6 losses."

Who knows who would have won the game if Geiser had been in left field? The sure-handed Geiser almost certainly would have held Sorn to a single and Knodle would have scored only one run.

August came to an end, and the American Legion's dream of its 16-team Invitational Tournament did, too. Not enough area teams signed up and the tournament was cancelled.

Community news continued to fill the front page of the Gazette. A story under the headline "AROUND THE TOWN" read as if it were a guide to home repair:

"The Chet Lands have painted their home on Howard Street.
"Wayne Adleman is painting his home on South Street.

"The J. D. Van Sickles have had a new roof put on their home on Howard Street.

"The Royce Burketts have had their home on south Center Street painted recently.

"The Frank (Ted) Haggertys are having a front porch taken off of their home on West Main Street in preparation of having the house painted."

Still smarting after their loss to Bullet Kirk, the Merchants called on their "jack-of-all trades," Bernie Figi, to fill in for Wilke on Friday night, Aug. 28. Figi responded by pitching a brilliant one-hitter as

Durand defeated Rockford's Gunite Foundry 7-5. Figi gave up only one single but was hampered by eight Merchant errors. Hines led Durand hitters with a solo home run and right fielder Bud Smith drove in two runs with a single.

Wilke returned on Sunday, Aug. 30, but gave up six runs and six hits in the first three innings as Carter-Gruenewald of Juda, Wis., handed the Merchants their seventh loss of the year, 8-4. Adleman with a home run and a single and Lloyd Mulvain with two singles led the Durand hitters.

The Merchants wound up the season early, on Wednesday, Sept. 2. They overcame a 6-2 deficit to defeat Rockford's Knights of Columbus 7-6 at Legion Field. After tying the game 6-6 in the sixth inning, Durand put a sudden end to the contest in the seventh. With one out, Hines was hit by a pitch. Wilke then slapped a single to right field and Hines scored when the right fielder juggled the ball.

The biggest local news of the year was the announcement that Durand's Pfc. Charles H. Long, who was shipped to the Korean War zone in January, was declared missing in action just six weeks later. A year later the War Department informed his parents, Henry and Mable Long, that Charles was presumed dead. At the time, the Army asked the Longs to send Charles' dental records. Doc Young, the dentist who helped lead the effort to build Legion Field in 1948 and kept meticulous records on his patients, complied. Fifty two years later, in 2006, after the Army negotiated with North Korea to obtain the remains of American soldiers, Doc Young's records made the positive identification. Long's remains were sent back to Durand and were buried in a grave site his parents had purchased in 1954 in St. Mary's Cemetery.

The Korean conflict still dominated the national news in 1953. On July 27, representatives of the United Nations, North Korea and China signed the Korean Armistice Agreement. By then, 25,604 Americans had been killed in the war. In baseball, Boston's Braves moved to Milwaukee and picked up dozens of Durand fans. The Braves, led by slugger Eddie Mathews and pitcher Warren Spahn, finished in second place in the National League with a 92-62 record. Even the addition of slugger Ralph Kiner couldn't prevent the Cubs from returning to their losing ways. They finished in seventh place in the National League with a 65-89 record. The New York Yankees won their fifth straight World Series, defeating the Brooklyn Dodgers four games to three. Johnny Mize and Mickey Mantle hit a total of five home runs and pitchers Allie Reynolds and Vic Raschi each won two games. The Rockford Peaches finished in fourth place with a 51-55 record in the All-American Girls Professional Baseball League.

The Merchants completed another great season, compiling an 18-7 record, even though Lloyd Mulvain and Jack Sharp played in only a handful of games. More impressive was Durand's 16-3 mark against Rockford teams. In three seasons where the record is nearly complete — 1950, 1952 and 1953 — the Merchants compiled a 40-8 record against Rockford teams, an unheard of 83 percent winning mark. The Merchants' five-year record jumped to 127 wins and 42 losses. Wilke once again was the staff pitching ace, despite missing a couple of games because of his new out-of-state job. He won 12 games and lost five. That boosted his four-year record to 77 wins and 22 losses, a 77 percent winning mark. Smith won four games and lost two and Figi finished the season at 2-0. Despite playing in only 12 games, Adleman was Durand's leading hitter again. Geiser, Hines and Figi also had very productive seasons.

What Merchant fans didn't realize was that they had watched Wilke pitch for the last time. He did not report for the 1954 season and, other than an occasional appearance at an old-timers game, did not pitch again for the Merchants. The "wheel" windup had taken its toll. Bothered by a nearly constant sore arm and faced with the demands of a new job in Indiana, Wilke retired in his prime at the age of 28. The record is not clear about how many games he won in his career. But pitching for the Durand Town Team and Irish Grove before joining the Merchants, Wilke most likely averaged at least 25 wins and 5 losses a year from 1945 to 1948 when the competition was much easier. Thus, he ended up with about 180 wins and 40 losses, an 81 percent winning mark. Durand would never have another softball pitcher as good.

CHAPTER 8

Slow Start, Fast Finish

When the Merchants became aware that star pitcher Roy Wilke was retiring and would not be available for the 1954 season, they started to search for a replacement. They didn't have to go far, only 10 miles south to Winnebago, where they recruited the Winnebago Legion's star pitcher, Russ Stringer.

Winnebago and the Merchants had played at least six times since 1949, each winning three games. Stringer beat Wilke in three of the six games despite Wilke pitching one of his career five no-hitters. Stringer was known as "Mr. Change-Up" because of his famous slow pitch. Like many other Merchants, he was a veteran of World War II and served with the Navy in the South Pacific. His family was among the original settlers of Winnebago, a village not much larger than Durand. He was 27 years old when he joined the Merchants.

Wilke wasn't the only Merchant missing in 1954. Four of Durand's best hitters — Wayne Adleman, Lloyd Mulvain, Jack Sharp and Johnny Hartman — did not play that year. Adleman was spending a lot of time in Colorado for his employer, Woodward Governor. Mulvain was now spending more time managing the Merchants than playing. Hartman, like Wilke, didn't play for the Merchants after 1953. For some unknown reason, Sharp sat out the 1954 season but he returned in 1955.

Stringer made his debut with the Merchants on Sunday night, June 13, against Rock City. Bernie Figi, playing second base, blasted a three-run home run with two outs in the bottom of the fifth inning to tie the game at 4-4. Minutes later, the game was called because of rain. Stringer gave up only four hits over the five innings but was hurt by two Durand errors.

First baseman Bill Alberstett, the former Durand High School basketball star playing his first year for the Merchants, led them in a come-from-behind victory on Friday night, June 18, as Durand defeated Juda 8-7 at Legion Field. Alberstett had three hits and outfielders Fred Geiser and "Bud" Smith chipped in with two each. Stringer probably pitched for Durand but the Gazette's two-paragraph game story mentioned no other details.

Durand lost its first game of the year on Sunday night, June 20, to Art's Friendly Service of Beloit, 3-2. Stringer gave up only one earned run and six hits but lost the decision on a pair of costly infield errors. The Merchants were held to four hits by Beloit's 18-year-old righthander, Stephan, whose first name was omitted by reporter Charles "Buzz" Stauffer in typical fashion. The game was highlighted by great defensive plays by Durand. Third baseman Jack McMahon handled nine chances with only one error and Geiser turned in a spectacular catch of a drive down the left field line.

The Merchants returned to their winning ways a week later with a 10-hit assault and beat Rockford Machine Tool 14-8 on Sunday, June 27 at Legion Field. With Machine Tool leading 6-5 in the bottom of the fourth inning, Durand unleashed a six-run barrage to ice the game. The big blows were a two-run home run by Figi and a solo home run by Bud Smith. Stringer, who gave up seven hits, and McMahon each had a pair of singles. Rookie Wayne Tracy, son of former Merchant manager Chuck Tracy, had a single and three walks and scored three runs.

A pattern was already emerging in the Gazette's coverage of the Merchants in 1954. Most of the game stories were only two or three paragraphs long and offered much less detail than the game stories of earlier years. The style and language used indicated they were still being written by Stauffer. But it was clear that Gazette owner-publisher John R. Van Sickle had won his argument: less space was now being devoted to the coverage of the Merchants.

At the same time, the Gazette devoted more space — five paragraphs — to the exploits of Durand's Little League team:

"Durand's Little Leaguers exploded with 40 runs in their first two starts as they dropped Davis 22-1 and Roscoe 18-1.

"Playing at the local field Thursday, June 10, Durand combined heavy hitting with tight pitching to outclass the Davis boys. Maury Ostergard and Ronnie Adleman split the pitching duties and the two registered 15 strikeouts in the five-inning game.

"Mike Waller was the batting hero with three singles and a grand-slam homer and Mike Mulvain clouted a triple and a fourbagger.

"Playing at Roscoe June 17, Durand's junior stars used the same combination of power hitting and three-hit pitching in gaining an 18-1 nod over the Roscoe youngsters.

"Adleman and Ostergard again teamed up on the hill, allowing Roscoe only three hits in the four-inning game. Gary Tracy, Rusty Sarver and Mike Mulvain paced the hitters."

The Gazette also reported on the auction of two one-room school houses. Walter Zissler purchased Sweet School on Moate Road for $1,350 and Merle K. Anderson bought Putnam School for $750. The Durand school district also announced the hiring of three new coaches. Marion Fox, the former basketball coach at Winslow High School, was hired to replace former Merchant Don Hubbartt as high school varsity basketball coach and teach American history and American problems. Sidney Felder, who had been teaching and coaching in Malta, was hired to teach in the grade school and coach the freshman-sophomore basketball team. Milton Truesdale, of Stoughton, Wis., was hired to teach in the grade school and direct all grade school athletics.

The paper failed to cover the Merchants' next four games but got back on track with coverage on July 15 of what it said was Durand's fourth one-run loss of the season. The Fairbanks Morse All-Stars of Beloit scored three runs on three Durand errors in the top of the seventh inning to edge the Merchants, 6-5.

A new pitching prospect appeared for the Merchants the next night, Thursday, July 16. Dave Hagen, a young fastballer who pitched in three leagues in Janesville, Wis., fired a one-hitter as Durand defeated Rockford's Woodward Governor, 5-3. He got all the help he needed from

Figi, who blasted a grand-slam home run in the sixth inning to erase a 2-0 deficit and seal the game for Durand. Hagen didn't allow a hit until he gave up a scratch single in the seventh inning. He struck out nine, including five in a row in the fifth and sixth innings. Stauffer wrote that "Hagen gave the crowd a thrill with his assortment of 'dipsydo' curves and fastballs, and it is planned to have him back within a week or two."

The Merchants, off to their slowest start ever, dropped to a 5-5 mark with one tie on Friday night, July 23 as they lost for the second time in a week to Fairbanks Morse All-Stars of Beloit, 8-7. All five losses were by one run. Stringer held Beloit to just three hits in the first five innings but was shelled for six hits and five runs in the sixth and seventh innings. Bud Smith led Durand with two hits.

Durand avoided dropping below the .500 mark two nights later by defeating Roscoe 11-8. Figi, back on the mound for the Merchants, survived a rough first inning, giving up three hits and a pair of runs. He then settled down and gave up only two hits in the next four innings. Durand scored three runs in the bottom of the first without a hit on three walks, an error and a hit batsman. The Merchants added four more in the fourth with center fielder Joe Hines' triple being the big blow. They iced the game in the fifth with three more runs on Alberstett's double and Jerry Mulvain's triple. Stauffer reported that "Jack McMahon, the Merchant's smooth-fielding third baseman, took over the mound duties in the sixth and displayed a tantalizing slow-ball over the final two innings."

Young Hagen was back on the mound for the Merchants on Friday, Aug. 6, but this time it was a disaster. He ran into trouble immediately and wound up allowing 10 hits, hitting seven batters and walking seven as Roscoe gave the Merchants one of its worst shellackings, 13-0. Ralph "Rosie" Rosenke held Durand to one hit, a single by Vernal Jones. Hagen's career with the Merchants was over in two games.

Durand rebounded on Sunday night, Aug. 8, when Stringer pitched a one-hitter of his own as the Merchants edged Art's Service of Beloit 2-1 in a game that lasted barely an hour. Stringer gave up a double in the first inning and an unearned run in the second on two Durand errors. He then retired the final 16 batters to face him. The Merchants, held to only two hits, scored their runs in the first inning without a hit on a pair of walks, an error and a passed ball. Catcher Jerry Mulvain played his first game at shortstop, his regular position when he played baseball, and handled eight chances flawlessly.

The Merchants then reeled off two one-run victories, first nipping Ridott 8-7 in eight innings on Friday, Aug. 13, and then edging St. John's Church of Rockford 3-2 on Sunday night, Aug. 15. Ridott threatened to win the game with single runs in the top of the seventh and eighth innings. Jones, who had pounded a homer earlier, singled in the tying run for the Merchants in the bottom of the seventh and Bud Smith's double and two errors led to the winning run in the bottom of the eighth. The Gazette story failed to mention who pitched for Durand. In Sunday's game, the Merchants collected only two hits, singles by McMahon and Jones. Durand scored all of its runs in the second inning on Jones' single, a walk, two errors and an infield out. Stringer held St. John's to five hits as the Merchants boosted their season record to 10 wins, 6 losses and a tie.

In a rare road trip, the Merchants then played two away games in five nights. They suffered their seventh loss at the hands of Leaf River, 4-1, on a mud-soaked field on Wednesday, Aug. 18. The two-paragraph game story failed to mention the names of any players. On Sunday, Aug. 22, Durand overcame a 6-0 deficit and defeated Club 51 at Beloit 9-8. The Merchants scored four runs in the third inning and five in the sixth to win the game. The Gazette reported that "Jack McMahon, the Merchants' talented infielder, turned in an outstanding defensive game and also wielded a big bat." But it didn't report on the number of hits by McMahon or any other Durand player. Stringer picked up the victory.

Between the road games, Durand returned to Legion Field and overpowered New England Banner's 4-H Club, 12-4, on Friday night, Aug. 20. Figi was on the mound for the Merchants and tossed a five hitter. But, once again, the game story lacked the names of any hitters and offered few details.

Many more details appeared in the Gazette's story about the opening of school. It listed the teaching and administrative assignments for the 1954-1955 school year: Gladys Geist, first grade; Marie Patterson, first grade; Irene Baker, second grade, Loretta Clark, second and third grades; Esther Panoske, third grade; Dorothy Green, fourth grade; Mary Butler, fourth and fifth grade; Genevieve Truman, fifth grade; Milton Truesdale, sixth grade and grade school coach; Sidney Felder, sixth grade and freshman-sophomore coach; Helen C. Johnson, seventh grade; Emmett Mulera, eighth grade; Gladys Luepkes, vocational homemaking; Harold Vale, vocational agriculture; Roman A. Baker, commerce; Donald Seymour, biology and history; Marion Fox, history and varsity coach; Ruth Downing, English; Glen Slabaugh, assistant high school principal, physical science and mathematics; Alex Las Casas, music; Paul G. Norsworthy, superintendent; Gerald Bliss, grade school custodian; Joe Andres, high school custodian and bus driver; and bus drivers Earl "Pete" Adleman, Jim Cowherd, Glenn Greene, Gilbert Dixon, Burdette Hanford and Almon Patterson.

The Gazette also announced that Durand's American Legion Gold Star Post No. 676 would hold its fifth annual horse show on Sept. 5 at Legion Field. The show featured 17 classes of horses and entertainment by the Arkansas Woodchopper, a county singing star for Chicago's WLS radio station. The annual horse shows were major fund-raising events to help defray the costs of operating Legion Field.

On Friday night, Aug. 27, the Merchants avenged two earlier losses at the hands of Fairbanks Morse All-Stars by defeating the Beloit team, 4-2. With the game tied 1-1 in the bottom of the sixth, Durand scored three runs on a walk, an error and singles by McMahon, Alberstett and Stringer. McMahon also led off the fourth inning with "a tremendous clout down the right field line" for a home run. Stringer gave up six hits while walking only one.

Durand ended August by picking up its 14th victory against seven losses and a tie on Sunday night, crushing New England Banner's 4-H Club for the second time in 10 days, 10-1. Jones paced Durand's attack with three hits, including a left-field home run. Stringer, who also homered, limited the 4-Hers to five hits. Center fielder Joe Hines made an outstanding play in the sixth inning when he caught a sinking line drive off the bat of Jon Dixon and fired a strike to second base for a double play. In addition to Dixon, the 4-H team included outfielders

Marv Meissen, Kerry Andres and Don Vormezeele, who with Merchant Bill Alberstett were members of the great 1953-54 Durand High School Bulldogs basketball team. After the Merchants, the Bulldogs, coached by former Merchant Don Hubbartt, were the second great Durand team that drew capacity crowds to every game. The starting lineup was Roger Sarver and Alberstett at guard, Ron Clint (who joined the Merchants in September 1954) and Vormezeele at forward and Meissen at center. Other team members were Wayburn Kelsey, Jon Dixon, Kerry Andres, Roger Larson and Dick Slabaugh. They compiled a 20-7 record, at that time the best in the school's history, and won the Stephenson County Conference championship.

Stringer chalked up two more victories on Friday, Sept. 10, and Sunday, Sept. 12. He came within two outs of a no-hitter before giving up two doubles in the top of the seventh inning as the Merchants beat Rock City, 4-2. He faced only 19 batters, one over perfection, in the first six innings. McMahon led Durand's hitters with a triple and a double and Figi added a home run. In a rare scheduled nine-inning game, Stringer hurled brilliant three-hit ball as the Merchants had little trouble defeating the Rockford Esquires, the city's all-Negro team, 7-2. Alberstett paced Durand's hitters with a triple, double and single and scored three runs. Jerry Mulvain, still playing shortstop, added three singles and Hines had a home run and a single. Durand registered two double plays, each started by second baseman Stu Weerda.

A week later, on Sunday night, Sept. 19, Durand and Stringer faced Rock City again, this time with its sensational young righthander, Gordon Dornink, on the mound. The thrilling game developed into a brilliant pitching duel, with the Merchants coming out on top 4-3 in 14 innings. Reporter Stauffer described the exciting match-up:

> "The Merchants were near-victims of a no-hitter over the regulation seven innings. Dornink, with two big outs behind him, suffered a temporary loss of control in the seventh, walking Jerry Mulvain and McMahon. Vernal Jones followed with a two-bagger for the first Merchant hit and Bernie Figi poled a single to send the game into extra innings, knotted at 3-3.

"From there until the fatal fourteenth, the game was a brilliant duel between two red-hot hurlers. Rock City threatened in the ninth with two out, but Stringer got Schwartz on a popup to escape damage. Alberstett singled with one away in the 10th but died on first as Dornink burned third strikes past Wallace and Clint.

"Hines opened the Merchant half of the fourteenth, reaching first on an error. Mulvain and McMahon followed with singles to load the bases. Jones, who had delivered the big blow in the seventh, came through with a solid single to send Hines home with the game ending run.

"Stringer's control proved the deciding factor of the contest. He gave up only eight hits and did not issue a walk until the 12th frame, while striking out 10. Dornink, on the other hand, encountered frequent trouble through his nine free passes but racked up a remarkable string of 15 strikeouts."

Other news in that week's Gazette included a report on the latest cases of polio, the dreaded disease of the era:

"Dennis Damon, son of the Dale Damons, is a patient at the St. Clare Hospital at Monroe, Wis. Dennis entered the hospital Saturday suffering from polio.

"Donald Sweet, also a polio patient, is improving at St. Anthony Hospital in Rockford."

The Merchants wound up their season the next week with two more victories. They exploded for 12 hits and hammered Juda, 12-2, on Friday night, Sept. 24. Jerry Mulvain led Durand with three hits and Alberstett and Figi each added two. Stringer pitched a six-hitter. The usual large crowd turned out for the final game of the season, on Sunday night Sept. 26, and cheered the Merchants to a 4-2 victory over a Cherry Valley Legion team that was led by a half-dozen all-tournament performers in the Rockford and Beloit leagues. That didn't faze Stringer, who gave up only a home run until the seventh inning, when Cherry Valley scored its other run on two scratch hits. Hines scored a run and doubled home the two decisive runs in the fifth inning.

The year 1954 was one of historic news. Dr. Jonas Salk, developer of the Salk vaccine to induce immunity to poliomyelitis, began inoculating school children in Pittsburgh. The Army-McCarthy hearings, led by Wisconsin Republican Sen. Joseph McCarthy, opened in April hell-bent on uncovering Communists in the military and U.S. government. Before the year ended, the Senate, in a special session, condemned McCarthy for making reckless allegations about "Communist conspiracies" and creating a climate of fear and mistrust among Americans. The hearings gave the English language a new word, "McCarthyism," the practice of making accusations of disloyalty without any evidence or proof. The Supreme Court tackled the race question head-on and declared unconstitutional segregation and the "separate but equal" facilities in public schools for Negroes.

In baseball, the Cleveland Indians stunned fans by ending the New York Yankees string of five straight American League championships. The Indians were led by sluggers Lary Doby and Al Rosen and four outstanding pitchers — Early Wynn, Bob Lemon, Mike Garcia and the great Bob Feller, nearing the end of his career. They then turned around and lost four games in a row in the World Series to the New York Giants, led by Willie Mays and two home runs by Dusty Rhodes. The Milwaukee Braves, in their second season and Hank Aaron's first, finished in third place in the National League with an 85-69 record. The Chicago Cubs, with Ernie Banks in his first season, continued their losing ways, finishing in seventh place in the National League with 64 wins and 90 losses. The Rockford Peaches, in the final year of the All-American Girls Professional Baseball League, went out with a whimper, finishing in fifth and last place with a record of 37 wins and 55 losses.

After a slow start to the season, winning six, losing six and tying one in the first 13 games, the Merchants won 14 of their last 16 games to finish the year with another very good record, 20-8-1, against good but less-than-great competition. Durand played the fewest big-city teams and the most small-town teams since 1948. Stringer gave Durand what it needed as a replacement for Wilke. The record is not clear —

the Gazette didn't report on nine games — but Stringer finished with Wilke-like numbers, probably 17-7-1. Bernie Figi was 2-0 and Dave Hagen was 1-1. Rookie Bill Alberstett was the team's leading hitter and got ample support from Vernal Jones, Jack McMahon, Jerry Mulvain and Figi. The Merchants' six-year record climbed to 147-50 with one tie, a winning mark of 74.2 percent. Despite the departure of Wilke and some other original Merchants, the future still seemed bright.

CHAPTER 9

Tragic Events

Pitcher Russ Stringer returned for a second season with the Merchants in 1955 and was joined by several rookies: Catcher Ray Michaelis, second baseman Roger Sarver, outfielder-pitcher Jon Dixon and outfielders Dick Koglin and Dick Slabaugh. In addition, Jack Sharp rejoined the team after a year's absence.

The Merchants opened the season not knowing that by the end of it they would be overshadowed by the biggest national story in Durand's history. They split a pair of games with two Rockford teams. Atwoods broke a 4-4 tie in the sixth inning with a pair of runs and defeated Durand 6-4 on Friday night, June 17. The Gazette story offered no other details. Two nights later, Stringer pitched a three-hitter as the Merchants evened their record at 1-1 by defeating National Lock, 4-1. With Durand leading 1-0 in the fifth inning, the ageless Vernal Jones, now 42 years old, broke the game open with a two-run home run. The Gazette's Charles "Buzz" Stauffer reported that "three newcomers shared the spotlight in the Merchant lineup — Catcher Ray Michaelis, outfielder Dick Koglin and second baseman Roger Sarver. All three looked good, both afield and at the plate."

Durand dropped below .500 the following Friday night, June 24, when Art's Service of Beloit scored five unearned runs in the fourth inning and defeated the Merchants, 11-6. Durand had 11 hits, including a two-run home run by Sharp, but failed to bunch them.

On Sunday, June 26, the Merchants repeated the 11-hit performance. This time it was enough to defeat Beloit's Central Market, 10-3. Stringer fired a five-hitter, striking out six and walking only one. Shortstop Jerry Mulvain paced the Merchants with three hits, including a double. Dixon and Jones each added two hits.

The Merchants continued their sizzling hitting, banging out 14 hits and crushing Rockford's Rural Youth team, 14-4, on Friday, July 1. It was a costly victory; Durand lost Stringer when he suffered torn ligaments in his left ankle while sliding into second base in the second inning. It appeared that he would be out of action for at least a week. Wayne "Red" Barron took over the pitching chores and held Rural Youth to five hits for the rest of the game while striking out six. Jerry Mulvain led Durand's attack with three doubles and Slabaugh had a triple, double and a single.

The Gazette story said newcomer Sid Felder added a two-run homer. But Felder said it never happened. "I never played one game with the Merchants," insisted Felder, the varsity basketball coach at Durand High School. Perhaps the Gazette was wrong. Or Felder may have forgotten. Regardless, Felder made his mark by coaching the other two great Durand athletic teams that drew capacity crowds for every game. His 1958-1959 basketball team surpassed the 20-7 record of the 1953-1954 team coached by former Merchant player Don Hubbartt with a 22-6 mark, including winning the state district championship. Starters on that team were Dave McCartney and myself at guards, Larry Damon and John Dickerson at forwards and Jim Walsh at center. Others on the team were Bill Haggerty, Mo Ostergard, Mike Mulvain, Ron Foss, Jerry Whisman, Jerry Clint, Jim Spelman, Eugene Laube, Shirl Fosler, Roland Boyer and Dennis Bottorf.

Three years later, Felder coached Durand's greatest basketball team, the 1961-1962 squad that lost its first and last games and won 25 in a row in between them. The team lost by one point to Freeport Aquin High School in its first game and went all the way to the semi-final game of the state regional tournament before losing to Rockford's East High School. Starters were Dave Alberstett and Gary Rapp at guard, Dick Stark and Steve Panoske at forward and Jim Stark, Dick's younger brother, at center. Others on the team were 6th man Bill Walsh, Ken Greene, Drake Erbe, Dave Meissen, Myron "Butch" Rafferty, Maurice Patterson and John Butler.

Back on the softball diamond, the Merchants boosted their record to four wins and two losses with a thrilling extra-inning victory on Sunday night, July 3, over Helland & Hein of Juda, Wis., 9-8. Michaelis carried the heavy lumber. He had a two-run homer in the fifth inning, doubled home the tying run in the bottom of the seventh inning and won the game in the ninth inning by driving in Dixon with a single. Sharp replaced Stringer on the mound and picked up the win even though he gave up 11 hits and nine walks.

And then, abruptly, the Gazette stopped covering the Merchants. No other game stories, or even bare scores, were published for the rest of the season. After being forced to shorten his stories about the Merchants and cover other local news, reporter Charles "Buzz" Stauffer had had enough. Despite being the town clerk, he quit his newspaper job and moved to Montana. Owner-publisher-editor John R. Van Sickle didn't replace him. Stauffer's leaving made it official: The heyday of Durand's greatest softball team was over. Gone were original Merchants Roy Wilke, Wayne Adleman, Lloyd Mulvain, Dick Highland, John Hartman and the Smith brothers, George and Bud. The Merchants would continue to field teams for the next several years but would not draw the capacity crowds of the past nor be as successful as the original team. An era had ended.

But news never ended. The biggest story in the history of Durand was breaking in 1955 and it was covered by the large daily newspapers in Rockford, Freeport and Beloit and eventually by the national media.

Poliomyelitis, the dreaded viral disease of the era that was characterized by inflammation of the brain stem and spinal chord and resulted in paralysis and sometimes death, struck Durand's Keron Walsh family. No one knew how or why polio struck or how it was spread. We were warned as kids not to sit next to an open car window or go swimming in the creek for fear of catching polio. The Walshes, who owned a farm about five miles northeast of town, had 14 children. Before their ordeal was over, 11 of them would be stricken by polio, five severely. The first was Rose Ellen, age 5, on Sept. 2, 1955. A week later polio assaulted the oldest son, David, 17. A day later, on Sept. 10, Edward, age 16, was stricken.

The town immediately rallied around the family. The parish priest at St. Mary's Catholic Church, the Rev. Joseph A. Driscoll, said a special mass on Sept. 11 for the family. It drew a huge crowd — even some non-Catholics — filling nearly every pew, the back of the church and even the side aisles, where people stood. The three altar boys — my brother

Dan, Bob Haggerty and Tom Dolan — were missing the fourth one, the stricken Dave Walsh.

At about the same time, the parents, Keron and Anne Walsh, were approached by station officials from WREX-TV, the CBS affiliate in Rockford, and urged to appear on the national quiz show, "Strike It Rich," to ask for prayers from the nation. Not wanting to leave their ill children, the Walshes recruited three representatives to make the trip to New York: Lorraine, their oldest child who had just graduated from Durand High School and a year later would be crowned the Durand Centennial queen; Margaret Walsh, the children's aunt who was Anne's sister and had married Keron's brother, Leonard; and Father Driscoll. The three of them flew to New York and appeared on "Strike It Rich" on Sept. 13, the same day that two more Walsh children — twins Joan and Julia, my classmates — became the fourth and fifth family members stricken by polio.

"Strike It Rich" was a CBS quiz show in which contestants were required to answer questions correctly to win up to $500. The show's host didn't ask Lorraine, Margaret or Father Driscoll any questions. He simply gave them the $500 after they told their story of a family besieged by polio and asked the nation to pray for all of them. Their prayers were answered. So much mail arrived in the next several weeks that rural carrier Floyd "Bump" Sarver, who often was the official scorekeeper at Merchant games, delivered the letters and cards full of money each day in a large clothes basket. More than $10,000, the equivalent today of $94,000, came from people all over the world.

About 30 years later, in the 1980s, Anne Walsh wrote a letter to her grandchildren describing the family's battle with polio. She entitled it "Tragic Events in 1955-1956-1957" and it told as only a mother could the gut-wrenching, riveting story of the Walshes' courage and faith:

> "1955 came and the children returned to school after Christmas. Winter passed and soon spring arrived, the flowers and trees all awakened, the birds returned and all the earth was glad. A wonderful breakthrough in researching Polio determined that children could be immunized by receiving the Salk vaccine. Children in Bernard's grade were to be the first to be immunized

after parents signed a permission slip. Bernard came home with a bright new 1955 penny to be used a souvenir of the first Polio immunization administered in our country.

"June came, bringing hot weather. The men working in the hay suffered terribly from the heat — at night they would be exhausted and complain of headaches from time to time. The heat continued into July.

"One morning we received a call from Marian Walsh to come over quickly. Uncle Jay had come into the cowyard and was lighting a cigarette when he fell to the ground lifeless. The rescue squad could not revive him. Doctors and the priest were called but he was not to be revived. Aunt Nita received the news at the home of one of her sisters in Indiana, where she had gone for a short visit. The family thought Jay's death was almost more than they could bear — so sudden, so beyond help. The day of Jay's visitation, our David complained of not feeling well — having a bad headache. He went to the doctor. He could not go to Jay's visitation, but was feeling better later and continued with helping with the harvest. The 4-H fair arrived and Dave and Ed showed their pigs and their cattle. Meanwhile, Bill Flynn had not been feeling well — had a temperature. His mother and dad asked David to show Bill's steer for him. He showed the steer for Bill, not thinking of himself, glad to help a friend. August passed, hot as July!

"The evening of September 2, Rose, age 5, complained of not feeling well. She couldn't really say how she felt but went to sleep and slept well. Next morning, September 3, 1955, was the first day of school. It was Tom's turn to enter first grade. After the children boarded the bus, I began to collect the clothes for a big wash. Rose started complaining of a terrible headache. She could not be comforted! I ran to the barn to tell your grandpa. We called Dr. Leonard. We dressed hurriedly, taking 3 year old Fran and 1¾ year old Molly with us to Rockford to take Rose to the doctor. The doctor said she was very ill — ordered a spinal tap at St. Anthony's Hospital. We waited, Grandpa, Fran, Molly, and me for the lab to read the results of the spinal tap. Soon Dr. Leonard came down the hall saying, 'Rose is in the first stages of Polio. The next 24 hours will be very critical. Take her to Township Hospital where she will be put in isolation.' I remember asking, 'Doctor, what about the other children? What can we do?' He said, 'We don't even know how Polio is spread. There is nothing we can do — just wait and see. There is no quarantine. The children should just go to school as usual.

"We took Rose to Township Hospital and handed her to a nurse who told us to wait in a certain place. After awhile she came back, handed us a brown paper bag containing Rose's clothes and told us we could not come in. The only way we could see her was to go to the outside until we came to the window which had steps up to a platform where we would be able to look in the window and see Rose in bed. She was to stay at least 7 days in isolation. We stayed for a short time, bid her goodbye and went home in a daze. On the way home I remember Fran or Molly reached on the dashboard of the car and took some gum which Rose had taken out of her mouth when she went into the doctor's office. She put it in her mouth before we could stop her. We kept returning to Township Hospital, climbing the stairs to talk to Rose, who wanted to come home, who complained of the shots the nurses gave her.

"Five days later, Dave complained that it felt like something was tingling in his back. He made me look to see if I could see anything — I could not. He went to bed, slept with Ed and awoke the next morning, September 9, with a headache and a stiff neck. He was so sick — on the way to the doctor he could hardly hold up his head. Right away the doctor tested him, asking him to lower his head until the chin could touch his chest. He could not do it. Again, we went to St. Anthony's for a spinal tap, which confirmed the fact that our 6 foot 2 ½ inch, 17 year old son, beginning his senior year at Durand High School, had Polio. We took him to Township Hospital, where we again waited until they handed us the brown paper bag containing his clothes, again saying we could not come in. We were to go outside to the steps leading to the same window. They put David in the same room with Rose. We looked in the window at our two children who a few days ago seemed healthy and happy. We knelt on the crude wooden steps and prayed God to help our stricken children. We left them to return to the rest of the family who were being cared for by Lorraine and other members of the family.

"The next day Edward decided to hunt for squirrels. He came back with one and asked me if I'd cook it for dinner the next day. I think, but I am not sure, that we were allowed to take Rose out of isolation over to St. Anthony's Hospital on Saturday, September 10. When we went to the door to get her, the nurses handed her out to us and I was shocked to feel her in my arms, limp — like a rag doll. The pediatric nurses and nun, Sister Grace, were ready with a stretcher to take Rose to her room where she was to remain for 3 months. I asked Sister Grace, 'How is Rose?' She replied, 'That depends on what you mean how is she?' She never answered my question but as soon as Rose was put in bed they put sandbags along her legs and back (this most likely was a treatment in which the sandbags were intended to immobilize her so that her limbs would not get deformed).

"I called the doctor to inquire for David. The doctor said, 'He is in a critical stage. I would prefer that he have no company.' Then I told him that when Ed got up this morning he complained that he felt very tight across his chest. He quickly said, 'Do not go to Township Hospital to see David but go straight home and bring Ed in for a spinal tap again at St. Anthony's.' We did as we were told, barely stopping to say hello to Rose, who seemed very quiet — her eyes larger than usual. Our whole mind and body wanted to go to see David, but instead we drove home, put Ed in the car and brought him to St. Anthony's, where a spinal tap was performed. Again we waited for the results. Dr. Leonard came down the hall once more to say that Ed had an even more severe case of Polio than either Dave or Rose. He sent us to Township Hospital for the third time in 8 days to deliver our second oldest son, age 16, a brilliant boy with sterling qualities, a boy who would never again go hunting, would never taste a meal made up of squirrel and whatever one eats with it.

"We waited again, at the door for the nurses to hand out his clothes in the now familiar brown paper bag. We were told to go to a different set of steps on the outside of the hospital and we could look through the window to talk to Ed. We visited awhile, then left him and mounted the steps outside Dave's window. The nurse told us how many of Dave's friends had been at the window to see him, not knowing the doctor's orders. Dave was burning up with fever. Grandpa Walsh and I hurried home to tell Father Driscoll that we wished him to say a mass for the children. I told him then that I didn't think I could stand it if we had to take Dave out of the hospital in the condition Rose was in.

"Mass was scheduled for the next morning. Before going, I called to ask how David was and should we go see him or go to mass? The doctor said that he was very ill but we might help him and the others more if we went to mass. The church was filled to the doors — people came to pray for us. Part way though the mass, I felt a tap on my shoulders. We were to go to Township Hospital immediately. David needed emergency surgery. We went and signed papers for a tracheotomy, but were not allowed in to see him or Ed. Again, we waited in the hall watching, as Doctor Glenn Smith entered, bottles of blood were wheeled by, and nurses scurried everywhere. Dr. Leonard was there and there was a priest summoned from St. Peter's church. Soon the familiar figure of Father Driscoll appeared and he spoke as he hurried into the isolation ward. Next a strange looking machine was hauled into the room, a machine that we were to become very familiar with — the iron lung, a cylindrical shaped thing with little glass windows across the top and a hole at the end. The machine could be opened the length of one's body. We were told later that Dave was placed in the iron lung because he could not breathe on his own and the machine would do it for him. The tracheotomy provided a hole in his throat into which a tube was inserted and a nurse stood by to suction out the fluid that kept accumulating — preventing Dave from breathing. He was drowning in his own fluids.

"Dave's body was enclosed in the iron lung and his head was pushed out the open end of the iron lung. He was completely paralyzed, not even able to swallow. When the doctors and priests came out, we were told nothing short of a miracle would get Dave on his feet again. We were told not to make any financial transactions which would incur expense. We were told that $25,000 would not begin to cover expenses caused by the effects of Polio. We were told to engage three private duty nurses for each child. Nurses around the clock! Meanwhile the news media entered the story, which was carried on national news. A woman from California called offering us money to help us out. Your grandfather thanked the lady and said we had Polio insurance — all we needed was prayers, lots of prayers.

"One evening when Keron and I drove to the hospital, two men left their cars and came over to us when we got out of our car. They were from WREX-TV and wanted us to fly to New York with Father Driscoll and appear on the program, Strike It Rich, all expenses paid and ask for prayers from the nation. We could not possibly leave our critically ill children. They suggested we send someone in our place. Finally it was decided that Aunt Margaret, Lorraine, and Father Driscoll would fly with a representative of WREX-TV to New York. They appeared on the program September 13, 1955.

"September 13 found us at Doctor Leonard's office with our 13 year old twins, freshmen in Durand High School. Again, we were sent to St. Anthony's Hospital for spinal taps for each girl. Again, we waited for the results of the spinal taps. Again, Dr. Leonard came down the hall saying that both girls are in the early stages of Polio and to take them to Township Hospital to be isolated for at least 7 days. We drove again to Township Hospital. The nurses took the girls to isolation. Again, we waited in the hall until the nurse came to the door with two brown paper bags holding Joan and Julia's clothing. Again, we were told we could not come in. We were told to go outside the hospital, where we were to climb the third unit of steps under the window of the room where Joan and Julia were admitted as the fourth and fifth member of our family stricken with Polio. We stopped at three different windows before we went home.

"We weren't home very long when we were called to Township Hospital. Both boys had taken a turn for the worst — not expected to survive the night. When we arrived at the hospital, authorities invited us into isolation, where we were given a room and asked to stay all night. The priest was called from St. Peter's again, both Dave and Ed were anointed and were given the last rites. Ed was placed in the iron lung and David was packed in ice in the iron lung — his temperature kept rising. When we entered his room the sight we beheld was beyond words. The huffing of the iron lung, the suction machine, the flushed face and wild eyes of our once happy and spirited young man, almost caused me to faint. The hushed voices of the nurses and the concern on their faces told us what we dare not ask. We were asked to come to a room where a young priest was waiting to offer us comfort and spiritual quotations, speaking highly of our sons who seemed to be such brave wonderful boys — a credit to their parents, etc. After the priest left, we were taken to a room where two beds were made up for us. We lay down but this was not a night for sleeping. The condition of the two boys had not worsened nor had it improved, but we felt we must go to Rose's bedside before going home. She was now going through rigorous physiotherapy with hot packs several times a day. She was still very weak, lying so still with sandbags still in place.

"The farmyard was crowded with cars of neighbors who came to do chores, religious groups who had come to pray, newspaper men, health authorities and relatives who had come to offer words of comfort and hope.

"The doctors were never able to do a spinal tap on Fran. She was so frightened! Nor on our baby Molly, but Fran had a light case of Polio leaving her with weak muscles in her neck from which she finally recovered after immersing her in a tub of hot water several times a day for many days.

"Letters came from all corners of the world. A fund was established at Central National Bank in Rockford with Arthur Johnson in charge. Many thousands of dollars were raised by friends and well wishers from all over.

"The last part of October a special ambulance was sent out from Chicago to transport David to Illinois Research Hospital. He was still totally paralyzed, could move his one big toe and turn his head. Edward was transferred to St. Anthony's Hospital, where he was given physical therapy, warm baths, etc. He could move his legs and had some use of his arms but he never made much improvement. Rose came home sometime around Thanksgiving. Ed remained in St. Anthony's Hospital and David in Illinois Research Hospital. The last part of December the doctors decided to admit Ed to Illinois Research along side of his brother, David, who was out of the iron lung and on a rocking bed which rocked up and down continually. (A rocking bed, like an iron lung, helped keep patients breathing and prevented them from choking on their own fluids).

"Rose's main trouble, the result of Polio, was that her muscles were weakened, especially her abdominal muscles which act as a guy wire to the spine. When they no longer supported her spine it began to curve badly. She was operated on to stiffen her spine, taking bone from her shin bones and fusing her backbone. This called for 2 major surgeries performed by Dr. Lyddon, a Rockford doctor. When the fusion did not hold, we took her to Dr. Blount in Milwaukee, who admitted her to Children's Hospital, Milwaukee. Rose had several operations, one 6 hours long. She wore a Milwaukee Brace. She had a transplant of fascia (a sheet of connective tissue binding together such body parts as muscles) to strengthen her abdominal muscles. Her body rejected it.

"The boys were still in Chicago. Joan and Julia stayed a month in the hospital and suffered no major complications, but had to undergo physiotherapy.

"One day while in Chicago, Dr. Saxton called me into his office and said they were sending our boys home for us to care for them. I was terrified! I was not a nurse and our closest doctor was over 20 miles away. He said, 'You know, now, more than most doctors know about Polio.' Their life depended on respirators and rocking beds. He was serious since they were beyond help. So we took our money, saved for later days, and built a room 20 x 24 with large glass windows. The boys were both to come home. The Polio foundation arranged to have two rocking beds sent out. A generator was installed in our basement to be used in case of a power failure. The room was finished, the rocking beds were there. We received a call on August 21, 1956, that our son, Edward, had died following a surgical procedure of having a tracheotomy. He and Dave were both in iron lungs at the time and Dave lay in the next iron lung knowing Ed had died, but was not able to raise a finger or a hand to wipe away a tear.

"The ambulance from Durand took Ed's body to Durand. It was later brought out to our farm home where a host of relatives and friends gathered. He was taken to St. Mary's for mass. He was buried in St. Mary's cemetery.

"Sometime later an ambulance took David home. He was put on the rocking bed where he stayed for about 9 months. He became ill in June 1957 and was taken to Chicago to Illinois Research Hospital and after many treatments and tests he died September 2, 1957, at age 19. His body was also brought to the house where services were held before taking him to St. Mary's church, Durand, for a funeral mass. He is buried beside his 17 year old brother, Ed, who died a year earlier from complications of Polio.

"This is the first and only time I have written about the tragedy in our family.

"I left out much of what happened between 1955 and 1957:

"— RKO movies came to our house to make a news reel.

"— Many prayers.

"— Many acts of kindness.

"— Many offers of blood.

"— Many neighbors who took turns bringing meals for the ones at home.

"— Many people who took us to Chicago.

"— I forgot to mention that Lorraine graduated from high school, May 1955.

"— She had her suitcase packed and was to enroll as a freshman at Edgewood College. She never went."

(For the next couple of years, Lorraine stayed home helping care for all the other children. Nevertheless, she found time to enter the contest to be queen of Durand's Centennial celebration in 1956. She wound up winning the title over six other candidates: June Raddatz, Sandra Bliss, Betty Keller, Pat Smith, Sandra Tallakson and Delores Davis.

Before a crowd of more than 1,000 surrounding town square park on July 12, 1956, Lorraine was crowned queen by Illinois Gov. William G. Stratton. Years later, Lorraine said she "was certain I was Centennial Queen because of our family's ordeal").

Anne's letter to her grandchildren continued:

"— My brothers and sisters who came to Chicago and stayed overnight.

"— Dave graduated from high school in 1956 in Illinois Research

Hospital. His superintendent and class came to the hospital.

"— I, also, did not mention that Ed tried for and got his driver's license on July 13, 1955.

"— Also, when I prepared the boys clothes, that they wore to the hospital, for washing them, I found David's 'Lucky Wheeler' in his pocket. (Silver dollar, which Uncle George got in Wyoming).

"— A picture of the sign posted near our farm 'A Future Farmer Lives Here — Ed Walsh' — appeared in the Army newspaper Stars and Stripes in Germany. "

— We were amazed to look out and see Ken Krienke doing the chores very early on Christmas Day morning. He knew your grandpa and I were going to Chicago to be with Dave and Ed. Ken did the chores many, many times with never saying a word.

"Grandma Walsh"

Thus ended Anne Walsh's heartbreaking account of her family's battle with polio and the death of her two oldest sons, David and Edward, who were the subject of dozens of short news items over the years in The Durand Gazette for their activities in school and the Durand 4-H club and at fairs showing their livestock. Of the nine other children afflicted, only Rose suffered any lasting effects.

When Ed died, The Rockford Morning Star saluted him and the family in an editorial:

"Death came Tuesday to Edward Walsh, 17, one of 10 children of the Keron Walshes of Durand stricken with polio last fall. Four Walsh children were not ill of the disease. Two are still receiving treatment.

"The plight of the family became known throughout the country. Prayers were offered for the recovery of the children. Sympathy for the Walshes was expressed in many ways.

"Edward, who would have been a senior in Durand High School this school year, made a courageous fight for life. He was a young man of promise. He was a member of the Durand 4-H club and the Future Farmers of America.

"Despite the tragic circumstances that attended the Walsh family, the members have been steadfast in their faith and courage. They certainly stand in the minds of most of us as exemplary in the face of misfortune."

Keron Walsh died 20 years later at age 74 on Aug. 12, 1976. Anne Walsh died at age 76 on Aug. 25, 1987. Both are buried next to their sons in St. Mary's Cemetery. Rose Walsh Landers, whose lifelong dream was to write a book about the family's polio ordeal, amassed a huge volume of material over the years. But she couldn't manage to find the time to write more than a few pages before being diagnosed in her early 60s with Primary Lateral Sclerosis, a slow form of ALS, or Lou Gehrig's disease. She recruited me and two of her sisters, Sue Walsh Cocoma and Julie Walsh Willkom, to help her write the book, "Triumph of Baker Road." It was published in 2016. Rose died at her home in Iowa City, Iowa, on Feb. 5, 2018 at age 67.

Anne and Keron Walsh, who lived on a farm about five miles northeast of Durand. Eleven of their 14 children were stricken with polio in 1955. Their battle against the disease became a national story, the biggest in Durand's history. (Photo courtesy of their oldest child, Lorraine Vormezeele).

Brothers Ed Walsh, left, and Dave Walsh. Ed died at age 17 of complications from polio on Aug. 21, 1956, and Dave died at age 19 on Sept. 2, 1957. (Photo courtesy of Lorraine Vormezeele).

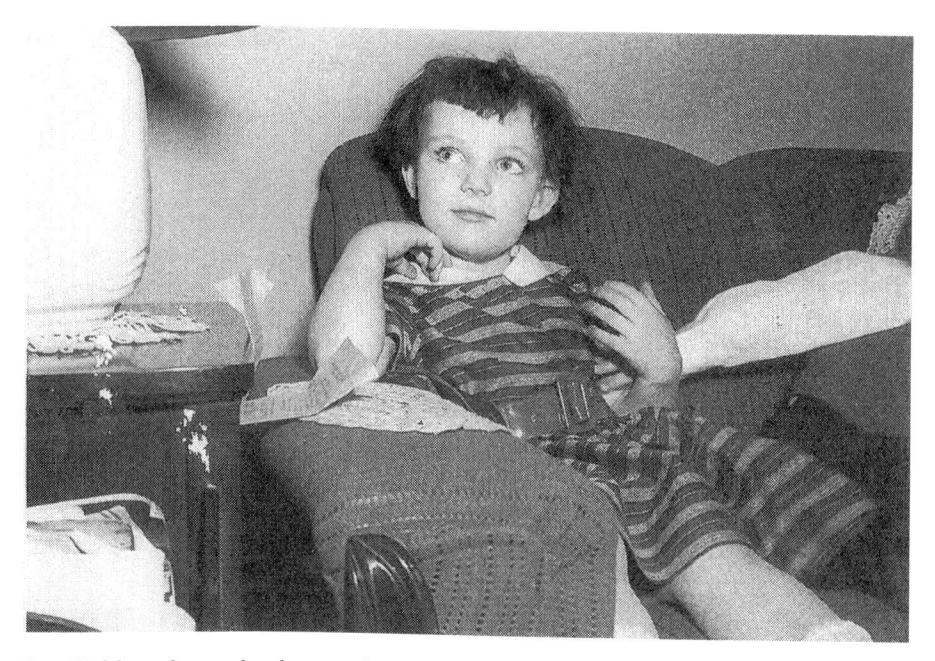

Rose Walsh on the couch at her grandparent's home in Beloit in 1956. (Walsh family photo).

Lorraine Walsh, left, Margaret Walsh and Father Joseph A. Driscoll board a plane for New York in September 1955 to appear on the television show "Strike It Rich."

TRAGIC EVENTS

Lorraine Walsh is crowned queen of the Durand Centennial by Illinois Gov. William G. Stratton in July 1956. (Photo by Dave McCullough/Dick Barron).

Queen Lorraine, center, with her court: From left, Sandra Tallakson, Betty Keller, June Raddatz, Sandra Bliss, Delores Davis and Pat Smith. (Photo by Dave McCullough/Dick Barron).

Above left, Daniel Ward Waller, foreground, president of the Centennial celebration, with Parker Zellers, director of the Centennial Pageant. (Photo by Dave McCullough/Dick Barron).

Above, right, Floyd "Bump" Sarver at the Centennial. Sarver umpired at first base at some Merchants' games when he wasn't the official scorekeeper. (Photo by Dave McCullough/Dick Barron).

Right, Merchant catcher Jerry Mulvain, left, and Tom Waller on the American Legion float during the Centennial parade. (Photo by Dave McCullough/Dick Barron).

ROY WILKE

PITCHER · DURAND MERCHANTS

CHAPTER 10

Whatever Happened to Them?

It is difficult to believe that more than half a century has passed since the Durand Merchants inaugurated Legion Memorial Field and captured the imagination of the little farm community. It's a cliché, but it seems like only yesterday I was watching them ring up victory after victory over the best teams from Rockford, Freeport and Beloit. But it has been nearly 70 years since I and my adolescent buddies chased down foul balls for a nickel. The last surviving member of the 1949 team, Wayne Adleman, died in August 2016. Here's what happened to all of them and some other important figures in the life of the team and the town:

ROY WILKE

Wilke, the star pitcher, along with the Mulvain brothers and Wayne Adleman formed the heart of the team. Although the records are sketchy during some years, they suggest that Wilke won about 180 games and lost 40, an 81 percent winning mark, from after World War II until his retirement at age 28 following the 1953 season. He was forced to the sidelines by a new job and a constant sore arm. He made a few appearances with the Merchants after that, pitching in old-timers games. My brother, Steve Waller, remembered one in the 1960s in which Roy faced a parade of young hitters and whiffed them one after another. "No one could even touch him," Steve said. "Many of us who were younger than you when he pitched for the Merchants and never remembered what he could do were amazed. The crowd behind the fence at home plate was four and five people deep just to watch the ball dance." Watching Roy and the Merchants and then playing competitive sports for all of my adolescence taught me several key values that guided me later in life: teamwork, sacrifice, persistence, and overcoming adversity.

Roy was born on Aug. 31, 1925. He joined the Hill Brothers Veneer Co. and Hammer Mill Paper Co. in Edinburgh, Ind., in 1953, eventually becoming the firm's chief of the buying department. He specialized in finding and buying walnut timber.

He was a man of few words. He spoke with a bit of a drawl, picking his words carefully. At first blush, he seemed to be an uneducated man, uncomfortable around those more intellectually bent. But it didn't take long to realize he was a street smart, savvy businessman who did not suffer fools gladly. He wrote off quickly anyone who broke his word or didn't work hard.

Steve Battern, who went to work for Roy at Hill Brothers in 1974, remembered him as a man of purpose and integrity. "I never saw him back down," Battern said. "Anything he said you could take as gold. He had a way of making difficult things look simple. He could make a deal even when it started out looking impossible.

"Roy was a stickler for detail. He didn't look as if he was paying attention but you'd discover later that he knew the smallest detail. He was an excellent teacher. He'd let you do what you thought was right. But if it didn't work, you'd hear from him or get a letter outlining the proper way to get the job done.

"Roy left the company in 1977 in a dispute with his manager, who tried to blame something on Roy when it was the manager's fault. Roy didn't put up with anyone who lied to him or didn't live up to his word. I replaced him and discovered the job he made look so easy was very difficult. I stayed another year but it wasn't the same without Roy."

Two years after leaving Hill Brothers, Roy started his own company, Wilke Timber Products, which bought trees, harvested them by sawing the logs into lumber and selling the veneer.

I experienced Roy's fondness of detail on several occasions. As a teenager I was hired one summer to paint his garage, located 50 yards behind his home on West Howard Street. Roy and his wife, Betty, who was as particular about how a job should be done as was Roy, checked on my work each evening and offered several "suggestions" as to how it might be improved. No garage ever got a more detailed inspection. Roy loaned me several hundred dollars to help with my college expenses and insisted that it be a business-like transaction with me signing loan papers each time I needed money. It was all legal and proper, though he never charged me interest. I incurred other debts while attending Millikin University but I put Roy at the front of the line and paid off his loans within 18 months after graduating.

Roy was a supreme outdoorsman and environmentalist. He was a breeder of Hereford cattle and loved a good steak. I shared his fondness for prime beef and each time he visited me at Millikin we would go to the Blue Mill Restaurant just off campus and order the biggest steaks on the menu. He loved boating, hunting and fishing and went on frequent trips, usually somewhere in the West. He also loved cattle shows, horse shows and rodeos and would take another of his nephews — my first cousin Jim Place, who like Roy was a cowboy at heart — with him to Denver and Kansas City to witness what little was left of the old West. He enjoyed amateur boxing and frequently attended the annual Golden Gloves tournament in Rockford. In his '70s, he swapped riding horses for riding snowmobiles. He and his wife Judy were members of the Durand Ditch Riders Snowmobile Club and took dozens of cross-country winter trips.

Loyalty mattered a lot to Roy. That's probably why he became very close to Mike Mulvain, who recalled his friendship with Roy:

> "My dad (Lloyd Mulvain) and Roy were neighbors and were like brothers. Roy was crushed when my dad was killed in an accident in 1956 while repairing electrical high lines. The bond between Roy and I became stronger after this tragedy. I think Roy felt a loyalty to my dad and transferred it to me.
>
> "Roy was a man of few words, and those few were direct and to the point. He had the reputation of a hard worker. Very few men could keep pace with him. Being a hard worker weighed heavily in Roy's evaluation of people. I found favor with him because

I was an ambitious, hard-working kid in his neighborhood. I mowed his lawn with a hand mower, shoveled his walk and driveway when it snowed, painted his house and did many other jobs around his property.

"I retired in 1990 from my first career after 29 years with Weyerhauser Paper Company and longed to start a small business. After much thought, I came to realize that I would love to do what Roy had been doing all of his adult life. In January 1991 I asked Roy if he would hire me and teach me the timber business. After a long pause, he said, 'I guess you can tag along with me if you want.'

"Our friendship became deeper as we traveled the back roads of Illinois, Iowa and Wisconsin looking at trees and logging operations. He taught me everything he could and suggested I purchase a portable sawmill so I could start sawing logs into lumber. I did, and began a sawing operation on leased property. My wife and I soon realized we would need our own place for the business to grow. But we were unable to find any suitable land for sale. I was complaining one day about it when Roy offered to sell us some land that he owned and was part of the old Waller farm about a mile north of Durand.

"It was the perfect location. We have been building our business on it for the past 16 years and now have a design center, a home, several kilns and woodworking buildings and eight employees. And we still have a sawmill. Without Roy's help, there would be no Mulvain Woodworks."

At age 21, Roy married my mother's half-sister, Betty Amundsen, on Jan. 15, 1947. They were close friends and socialized regularly with my parents and Marsden and Naomi Place, my mother's other sister. Shortly after joining Hill Brothers, Roy and Betty moved to Pekin, a small city of about 30,000 about 175 miles south of Durand in Central Illinois. I remember visiting them and having a difficult time sleeping because it was the first time I had ever heard police sirens at night. After a couple of years, they moved back to Durand.

Betty died of heart disease at age 56 on Jan. 8, 1983. Their marriage produced no children. A year later, Roy married Beverly Geiser, the former wife of ex-Merchant left fielder Fred Geiser. She died three years later at age 54. Both Betty and Beverly are buried next to Roy in Durand Cemetery. Slightly more than a year later, on June 7, 1988, Roy married Judy Schulte of Argyle, Wis.

In 2001, Roy had a bout with bladder cancer. After about six months of treatments, his oncologist, Dr. Greg Medis, told him that he was cured and that the bladder cancer would never return. But he predicted that cancer in some other form would come back in four to six years.

Unfortunately, he was right. Severe liver cancer showed up in Roy in February 2005. In late July, during a visit to Dr. Medis, who had become accustomed to Roy's reserved ways, asked him, "How do you feel about all of this that's happening to you?" Roy replied in his drawl: "Doc, I've lived my life the way I wanted to. I made my own choices. I have no regrets." He died about a month later, on Sept. 2, 2005.

JERRY MULVAIN

Jerry Mulvain, the Merchants' catcher in the early years and shortstop in the later ones, was a terrific ballplayer and loved baseball as much as softball. He played fast-pitch softball for 26 years, following his discharge from the Marines in 1946 until he quit at age 46 in 1972. Jerry served in Guam and during the invasion of Leyte Island in the Philippines during World War II. His three brothers, Virgil, Rollin and Lloyd, also served in World War II.

Softball and baseball weren't the only sports at which Jerry excelled. He was a star basketball player in high school where his leadership qualities became apparent: he was elected president of his class his junior and senior year. He, as well as fellow Merchants Fred Geiser and Bud Smith, was an outstanding bowler.

He married Juanita Damon, the daughter of Ernest and Fern Damon, on March 1, 1947, in Durand. They had two daughters, Vicki Kocher of Durand and Linda Wise of Rockford, three grandchildren and five great-grandchildren.

Jerry worked a year for Roy Wilke, cutting logs. "It was good working for Roy," he said. "He wanted things done the right way. As long as you did that, he was good to work for. We were close friends." He then worked 14 years for Durand Township, mainly on area road jobs. After three years working on electrical high lines, Jerry had a six-month stint at National Lock. But he loved the outdoors and returned to his road work, this time for the Winnebago County Highway Department, from which he retired after 25 years.

A man with a melodious voice, he sang at funerals all of his adult life. He got his start by singing as a youth in the choir of Durand's United Methodist Church. His tenure as the bass singer with Hometown Harmony was nearly as long as his softball career — 23½ years. With Betty Greene at soprano, Arlene Fischer as alto and a variety of tenors, the group had 342 performances of barbershop, gospel, hymns and seasonal music, entertaining people at nursing homes, retirement centers, churches, birthdays, anniversaries, wedding parties, picnics and fairs. He also sang at more than 300 funerals, including those of Merchant teammates Roy Wilke and Jack Yaun. Unlike most other Merchants, he didn't serve on any community boards —"I was too busy playing ball." But he served the community by coaching Little League teams and, for 25 years, the Durand Cherubs women's softball team. He was a close friend of the Gazette's Charles "Buzz" Stauffer and for a few years bowled in Durand's leagues with him. Jerry died on Oct. 11, 2013 at the age of 87. Juanita, the family's biggest sports fan who watched hundreds of ball games played by Jerry and then by her children and grandchildren, died 4½ years later on April 29, 2018 at age 90.

LLOYD MULVAIN

Like his younger brother Jerry, Wayne Adleman and Jack Sharp, slick-fielding shortstop Lloyd Mulvain was a great hitter. He, too, was a Marine and served in the 2nd Marine Division in the decisive battle of Iwo Jima during World War II. He was a key Merchant player until 1953, when he became the player manager and often left himself out of the lineup. Lloyd was also a great baseball catcher, good enough to have played in the minor leagues and, possibly, the major leagues. But he gave up any notion of a baseball career and started a family instead. At age 19, he married Clara Lou Blome in Dubuque, Iowa, on July 24, 1939. They had two sons, David and Mike. Lloyd began working as a lineman with Central Illinois Gas and Electric Co. in 1942. He was active in the community, where he was a member of the Methodist Church, coached Little League baseball teams and served on the Durand village board and as chairman of the board of directors of the Durand Centennial Association.

But then the unthinkable happened. He was killed on April 2, 1956, as he was attempting to restore the current to a farm house near Shirland. He grabbed the 6,900-volt line after climbing a utility pole and was electrocuted as he touched a grounded bolt with his other hand. His partner, Durand's Paul Downing, and Rockton police removed him from the pole and took him to Beloit Municipal Hospital, where he was pronounced dead on arrival. His survivors included his three brothers — Jerry, Virgil and Roland — and his sister, Mrs. Lilas Tracy. The entire town was devastated. He had been my Little League coach and his son Mike was one of my best buddies. His death hit hard for all of us.

WAYNE ADLEMAN

Wayne Adleman was born on Dec. 23, 1919. He was an outstanding hitter and the team's best slugger. He originally played third base but switched to shortstop and occasionally second base when Jack Sharp joined the team and Lloyd Mulvain began playing fewer games when he became the player-manager. Adleman frequently fielded ground balls with one hand, unlike Lloyd who always fielded them with two. Like Lloyd, he also played baseball. He thought the Merchants' best infield lineup ever was when he played second base with Dick Highland at first base, Lloyd Mulvain at shortstop and Sharp at third base.

Adleman graduated from Durand High School in 1937 and married Lois Stoll of Durand on Sept. 4, 1940. He joined the Navy in 1944 and was on a ship that never saw action in World War II and was discharged in 1946. He played regularly with the Merchants until 1954, when he began playing sparingly. Except for a couple of years working as a painter for the Illinois Paint Co. in Rockford, he worked for the Woodward Governor Co., which among other things designed and manufactured fuel controls for aircraft engines. His working colleagues included George Smith of the Merchants. The company was one of Rockford's largest, employing more than 2,000 people in the 1940s and 1950s. Adleman's Merchant career was finished well before 1957, when Woodward Governor promoted him to chief of the quality control inspection department and transferred him to its Ft. Collins, Colo., operation. He left Woodward Governor in the mid-1960s to sell real estate and insurance in Colorado but returned to Rockford and Woodward Governor in 1970, where he retired 10 years later.

During Wayne's tenure with the Merchants, the constant debate at Bill Steward's barber shop about who was the best ballplayer on the team most often wound up in an argument over Wayne, Jerry Mulvain, Lloyd Mulvain or Roy Wilke.

Wayne, who died Aug. 29, 2016, in Sun City, Ariz. at age 96, was the last surviving member of the Merchants' 1949 team, which compiled its greatest record of 34 wins and 6 losses. Survivors included his wife, daughter Pat Olander (my high school classmate), sons Ron and Gary, 6 grandchildren and 10 great grandchildren.

JACK SHARP

Jack Sharp, a terrific third baseman and occasional pitcher, was the equal of Adleman and the Mulvain brothers as a hitter. In fact, Adleman thought that Sharp and Lloyd Mulvain were the team's best hitters. Sharp's arm was so strong from third base that he could nearly knock down the first baseman. The record isn't clear but Sharp probably joined the Merchants in 1952 after serving in the Air Force during the Korean War. What is clear is that he was the best all-around athlete on the team. That was reflected later in his life when he participated in the Senior Olympics at Madison, Wis. He was still playing for the Merchants in 1955, when the Gazette stopped covering the team after the first six games.

Born on Aug. 3, 1930, he lived most of his life in the Shirland area, where he farmed. Shirland was about seven miles east of Durand and was even smaller, with a population of about 300. Like Wilke, he loved the outdoors and was an avid runner and fisherman, leading several Canadian fishing trips. Sharp married Julia Potter in Rockton on Nov. 17, 1951. They had two sons, Allan and Joel, four daughters—Amy, Rebecca, Joanna and Jeanne — and five grandchildren. He was active in the community, where he served on the administrative board of the Shirland United Methodist Church. He also was a 4-H leader, a Boy Scout advisor, a boys' basketball and softball coach and a member of the Winnebago County Farm Bureau. He died suddenly at age 57 on June 5, 1988, while running along Boswell Road in Rockton.

DICK HIGHLAND

Dick Highland was an excellent first baseman and a very good hitter with considerable power. He was a mainstay in the 1949 and 1950 seasons and probably played in 1951, though there is no record for that year. He had retired from softball by 1952, when he was 32 years old.

He was born on Dec. 31, 1920, and lived his entire life in the Durand area, as did most of his eight brothers — William, Thomas, Bernard, Robert, Paul, John, James and Joseph — and three sisters — Mary, Ann and Jane. Highland worked for the Illinois Department of Agriculture before purchasing in 1955 the Durand Feed and Seed Co. on Center Street just south of the railroad depot. He operated the store until he sold it to the Winnebago Service Company in 1964, when he became their store manager until 1975. He married Marcia Hartman, the sister of second baseman John Hartman, on Feb. 23, 1946. They had four sons and four daughters — Thomas, Daniel, David, Patrick, Susan, Mary Jane, Ann and Lisa — and five grandchildren.

Highland also was active in the community. He was a member of St. Mary's Catholic Church and the Knights of Columbus. He served a term as president of the Durand Businessmen's Association and was a member of the original Durand Sanitary District, the Durand Zoning Board and the Winnebago County Farm Bureau. Like Jack Sharp, Highland died at a young age, 56, on Jan. 21, 1977, in Rockford Memorial Hospital.

BOB HIGHLAND

Bob Highland, Dick's older brother, was an excellent second baseman but had his softball career abruptly ended in 1948 when he broke his ankle in a game in which an opponent slid into him at second base. He remained a huge fan of the Merchants. He married Margaret Bentley in Durand on November 17, 1945, and had a son, Robert, two daughters, Joan and Mary Beth, and four grandchildren. Highland served in the Army in World War II in the European theater and was awarded a Purple Heart after being wounded at Anzio beachhead during the Italian campaign. He delivered oil and kept the books for Spelman DX and Sunoco service stations for more than 40 years. At the same time, he owned with his wife and sister-in-law, Ramona Bentley, the Bentley and Highland Grocery Store on Center Street on the town square. He was a member of St. Mary's Catholic Church and Durand's American Legion Gold Star Post No. 676. He died at age 78 on Oct. 12, 1998, in Durand's Medina Nursing Home after a lengthy illness.

JOHN HARTMAN

John Hartman was a terrific successor to Bob Highland at second base. He was a very good hitter and glove man from 1949 until 1953, except for when he was in the Army. He was born on May 9, 1929, graduated from Durand High School in 1947 and he lived all of his life in

Laona Township, adjacent to Durand Township. He married Kathryn Yaun, the sister of Merchant right fielder Jack Yaun, on Feb. 21, 1953. They had three daughters, Holly, Heidi and Jill, and five grandchildren. Hartman worked for many years at the M&M Grocery in Durand and was a part-time farmer until he retired in 1991. He then worked 10 years for the Lake Summerset Association. He served in the Army Infantry during the Korean War and was a member of the American Legion Gold Star Post No. 676. He was very active in the community, serving as president for 22 years of the board of Fire Protection District No. 1 and on the Winnebago County Board and Winnebago County Planning Commission. He was a Laona Township Supervisor and a member of the Winnebago County Farm Bureau for several years. He died at age 75 on Sept. 8, 2004, in Freeport Memorial Hospital.

FRED GEISER

Left fielder Fred Geiser teamed up with center fielder Joe Hines as fixtures in the outfield for several years. Geiser wasn't as fast or as acrobatic as Hines but was an excellent left fielder nonetheless. Few balls ever got past him and he made countless dazzling catches of balls hit into the row of cars parked along the foul line. He played for the Durand town team in 1947 and 1948 before the Merchants were formed and like Jerry Mulvain played long after the other original Merchants had retired.

A great bowler, he is a member of the Durand Bowling Association's Hall of Fame. He won several championships over the years, including mixed team tournaments with partners Marilyn Place and Shirley Adleman. Much of his competition came from his Merchants' teammates Jack Sharp and Keith "Bud" Smith. Fred could have won more tournaments but he gave up the game at a somewhat early age.

Fred was a close friend of Durand Gazette reporter Charles "Buzz" Stauffer and met him often on Sunday mornings at Lionel "Curley" Weaver's home to play double pinochle. Fred loved playing cards and was great at almost any card game. He was terrific at euchre and later in life became accomplished at Pegs & Jokers, a game he learned with his wife in their winter stays in Arizona.

"He was sharp as a tack and was two plays ahead of everybody else when you played cards with him," recalls Mo Ostergard. "He could remember every card you played, even two hands back."

Fred enlisted in the Navy in 1945, winding up in the Seabees and participating in the next two years in salvage and construction projects in Japan and Southeast Asia.

He married Beverly Place on April 16, 1949, and they had five children: Carol, Gary, Linda, Randy and Debbie. Following a divorce, he married Dorothy Yates on March 10, 1986.

Fred was noted for his strength and stamina — well into his 80s he could still outwork most men in their 20s. He lived and worked on the family farm about a half-mile north of Durand on Crowley Road from 1936 until he died on Aug. 20, 2015 at age 87. He was survived by his wife, five children, 15 grandchildren and 20 great grandchildren.

JOE HINES

Joe Hines was a pitcher's best friend. He was as fast as lightning and patrolled center field as if he owned the land. Nothing got by him. No runner dare try to take an extra base on him or he would uncock his bazooka-like arm. He was a great base stealer and bunter and an overall very good hitter. He was the best softball center fielder I ever saw. Hines was born on March 14, 1925, graduated from Durand High School in 1942 and farmed all of his adult life in the Durand area. He married Kathleen Hartman, another sister of John Hartman, on Nov. 29, 1947. They had eight children — James, Richard, John, Mike, Doug, Janet, Mary Ann and Joan — and 10 grandchildren. He was a member of St. Mary's Catholic Church and the Winnebago Farm Bureau. He died at age 65 on July 13, 1990, in St. Clare Hospital, Monroe, Wis.

JACK YAUN

Jack Yaun was one of several players who roamed right field for the Merchants. He was a solid hitter and fielder but played for only a few years, missing the 1951-1952 seasons while serving in the Army's 69th Field Artillery Battalion of the 25th Division during the Korean War. Born on Dec. 28, 1924, he lived most of his life in the Durand area. He farmed for years and then served from 1962 to 1971 as a highway maintenance worker and driver's license examiner for the state of Illinois. After that, Yaun joined Chilton Realty in Durand as a salesman. A 1943 graduate of Durand High School, he married Betty Jean Ehlert on Nov. 27, 1953, in Freeport. They had a son, Steve, and a daughter, Jacki, three grandchildren and a great grandson. He was very active in the community, serving as a member and president of the Durand Board of Education and a member of the Winnebago County Board of Supervisors and the Winnebago County Farm Bureau. He also served as a Laona Township precinct committeeman and was a 50-year member of the Durand American Legion Gold Star Post No. 676 and of the Durand Masonic Lodge. For more than 50 years, he and his wife were members of a card club that included Jerry and Juanita Mulvain. At age 81, Yaun died after a lengthy illness on Oct. 19, 2006, at his home in Brodhead, Wis.

THE SMITH BROTHERS

George Smith and his older brother, Keith "Bud" Smith, shared right field duties with Jack Yaun and Wilke when he wasn't pitching. George was a solid player but Bud was a better hitter and played more often than George, who was a key leader in the building of Legion Memorial Field in 1948. Both were born in Rockwell City, Iowa, Bud Jan. 16, 1922, and George on Oct. 1, 1923, and both lived most of their lives in Durand. Each served in the Army during World War II, Bud in the Transportation Corps in France and George in the Medical Corps in Burma. Bud was truck driver for C.A. Smith Trucking Co. in Durand until 1950, when he joined the Barber-Coleman Co., which manufactured parts for heating and air conditioning systems. He worked for the firm in Loves Park, a suburb of Rockford, until he retired in 1977. He was an avid model airplane builder and won several awards, including first place at the 1980 Winnebago Sports Modelers Show and third place at the 5th annual Chicago Expo. He loved his cars; as a youngster I remember Bud cruising around town on Sundays in his new Chevy. He always had a new car, because he bought one every year. He died on Oct. 19, 1990, in his home, leaving a daughter, Nancy, and two grandchildren.

A 1942 graduate of Durand High School, George married Myrta Jean Bentley, a widow who had three children, on Aug. 20, 1960. He worked for more than 40 years as a machinist at Woodward Governor Co. in Rockford. He was a member of Durand's United Methodist Church and the boards of the Durand State Bank and Durand Sanitary District. He also was a member of Ducks Unlimited and, like Bud, of the American Legion Gold Star Post No. 676. George died at age 75 in his home on Oct. 14, 1998.

WAYNE "RED" BARRON

Another right fielder, Red Barron also played left field when Geiser was absent and pitched when Wilke needed a rest or was on the sidelines with a sore arm. Barron was a good outfielder and hitter, and a very effective pitcher when he wasn't wild. His temper was as fiery as his red hair and derailed some of his mound stints. He was born Jan. 9, 1924, and lived all of his life in Durand. He served in France and Germany in the Army during World War II and was wounded in the Battle of the Bulge, for which he received the Purple Heart. After the war, he worked for 13 years for Greenlee Brothers in Rockford, which manufactures professional tools, and several years for Durand Plumbing and Heating before becoming self-employed. He was a member of the American Legion Gold Star Post No. 676 and the Ross-Pearson VFW Post 5149. He died after a lengthy illness on June 17, 1992, at the V. A. Hospital in Madison, Wis., leaving a son, Michael, and two grandchildren.

BERNIE FIGI

Of all the Merchant right fielders, Bernie Figi rivaled Barron as the best. He was a very good hitter and outfielder. His real value was his ability to play nearly any position — left field, right field, first base, second base, third base or pitcher. Like Barron, he filled in on the mound for Wilke and won some key games. He played for the Merchants starting in 1950 for about five years and also played for the Helland Heins team from Juda, Wis., with three brothers, Boyd, Roy and Ray Figi. Bernie was born July 14, 1922, into a farm family near Monroe, Wis., and after graduating from Juda High School in 1939 farmed for most of the rest of his life, working for brothers George and Jay Walsh before buying his own farm in 1965 on Walnut Grove Road north of Davis. A year earlier, his wife, Rosemary, and two of his children were killed when their car was hit by a vehicle that ran a stop sign. A daughter, Denise, survived. He then married Joyce Lohmeier Meinert. Figi also was active in civic affairs, serving on school boards in both Durand and Juda and for 25 years on the Davis Fire Department. He also served 20 years on the Tri-District Ambulance Service. Now 96 years old, he and Joyce together have seven children — Denise, Walter, Nancy, Bruce, Dennis, Patty and Pam — 11 grandchildren and 2 great-grandchildren. The Figis live in their home on Stateline Road, just north of their farm, which they sold to Joyce's son, Dennis Meinert.

JOHNNIE SMITH

No relation to George or Bud Smith, Johnnie Smith pitched from 1951 to 1953 for the Merchants. At 6 foot 3 inches tall and weighing more than 200 pounds, he was an imposing figure on the mound. His pitches weren't very fast but he put a lot of spin on the ball, causing batters to hit pop-ups and ground balls. Born March 31, 1917, he lived most of his life in the Durand area. Except for about a dozen years when he worked for Rocky's Tap in Rockford, he was self-employed as a farmer. He married Harriet Lorenz of Beloit, Wis., on July 14, 1939 and they had six daughters — my classmate Judith Osborne, Kathleen Scheck, Patricia Albrecht, Susan Ballard, Laurie Smith and Betty Ryhner — and a son, Johnnie, and nine grandchildren. He died of a sudden illness at age 67 on April 23, 1984, in Rockford Memorial Hospital.

JACK MCMAHON

At age 16 in 1949, Jack McMahon became the youngest player ever to appear in a Merchants' uniform. He was an excellent infielder and hitter and with Hines the fastest man on the team. He was an even better baseball player, perhaps the best one ever to come from Durand. Born April 29, 1933, he left Durand in 1950 for Corpus Christi, Tex, where he graduated from high school and signed a contract in 1951 with the Corpus Christi Aces, a Class B team in the Gulf Coast League. He was optioned to the Odessa Oilers, a Class C team in the Longhorn League and played there and with some other minor league teams. It's not clear how far he advanced in the minor league system, but there is no record indicating that he played professional baseball after 1951. A Navy veteran, he played softball off-and-on the next couple of years with the Merchants and a few years later for the national champion Aurora Sealmasters. A first marriage, to Bernice Lohmeier, produced a son but ended in divorce. After that, he married Mary Lemanski of Kewanee, Ill., and they had two daughters. McMahon lived in Rockford, where he was a mail carrier for the U.S. Post Office. He later moved to Geneseo and then to Dubuque, Iowa, before eventually moving to Florida. He suffered from Alzheimer's disease the last two years of his life and died of a heart attack at age 72.

DON HUBBARTT

The former Durand High School basketball coach, Don Hubbartt filled in at catcher and first base for the Merchants from 1949 to 1952. He was a good hitter but was hampered by bad knees, the result of his service in World War II. Born Sept. 30, 1923, he graduated from Taylorsville (Ill.) High School in 1941 and enlisted in the Air Force, where he served as an aerial gunner on several missions over Europe on B-17 bombers. He was awarded the Air Medal with oak leaf clusters and the Distinguished Flying Cross and was discharged for medical reasons. Hubbartt married Mary Jo Ware of St. Andrew, Fla., on Aug. 24, 1948, and graduated from the University of Illinois in 1949, when he started teaching and coaching at Durand High School. He also was the assistant principal. In 1952, he organized the first Durand Holiday Tournament, the annual high school basketball invitational tournament held during the Christmas holidays. Hubbartt ended his teaching career in 1956 when he joined the Barber-Coleman Co. as a production engineer. He worked there until he retired in 1984. He and his wife moved in 1957 to Winnebago, where he became active in civic affairs. He served on the village board and as president of the school board and Winnebago Community Council. He was a member of the Winnebago County Board of School Trustees and the Winnebago Presbyterian Church. He was a 52-year member of Durand's American

Legion Gold Star Post No. 676. He and his wife, who taught at Durand Grade School in 1949 and 1950, had two sons, Mark and Bruce, a daughter, Barbara, and two grandchildren. He died at age 77 on Oct. 7, 2000, in Rockford Memorial Hospital.

VERNAL JONES

Vernal Jones, born Dec. 14, 1913, was 38 years old when he joined the Merchants in 1952. A first baseman, he was a terrific hitter at any age. He played well into his 40s, at least until 1955. He lived all of his life in Avon (Wis.) Township, about 30 miles northwest of Durand. He married Edith Eleanor Perry on Sept. 26, 1935, in Freeport, Ill., and they had six sons — Jerry, Ronald, Michael, Richard, Scott and a boy who died in infancy — and three daughters — Donna, Nancy and Patricia. A farmer for many years, he also worked for Beloit Corporation for 25 years before retiring in 1976. He was a member of the Avon Community Church, the Newark Gun Club and the Beloit Corporation Quarter Century Club. He died at age 68 on March 3, 1982, at University Hospitals in Madison, Wis.

RUSS STRINGER

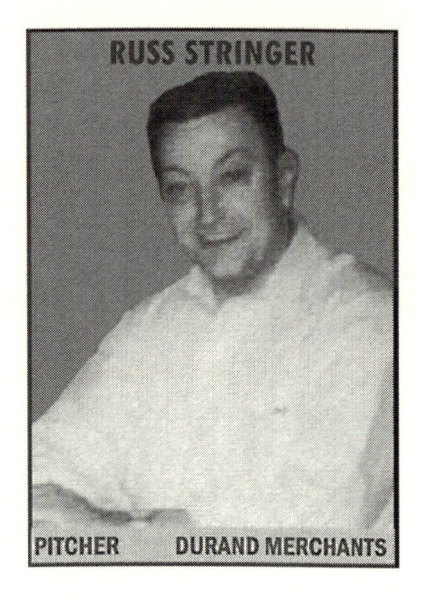

Russ Stringer, known as "Mr. Change-Up" for his famous slow pitch, replaced Wilke as the Merchants main pitcher in 1954, winning 17 and losing 7, with one tie. He stayed for the 1955 season but for most of his career he pitched for the Winnebago team. Born Dec. 8, 1926, he served in the Navy on the aircraft carrier USS Saidor and saw action during World War II in the Atlantic and Pacific theaters. He was fastener engineer and worked for National Lock Co. of Rockford for nearly 39 years and five more years for the W.G. Jackson Co., retiring in 1990. Stringer also was a renowned artist, known for his life-size murals of local families and historical buildings. His family was among the original settlers in Winnebago and he grew up in the oldest house in the village, at 105 S. Elida St. He married Janet Marie DiGvonni on May 9, 1964, in Pecatonica. He was a member of Winnebago's United Methodist Church, American Legion Post 197 in Pecatonica and the Gun & Pellet Club in Rockford. He and his wife had two daughters, Amy and Laurie, and a granddaughter. He died at age 67 of complications from diabetes and heart disease on June 25, 1994, in Rockford Memorial Hospital.

KEN DITZLER

Ken Ditzler rarely missed a Merchants' game as a youngster but played only one full season for them, in 1953 after he graduated from Durand High School. He was a slick-fielding third baseman who saw plenty of action because Sharp played only a few games that year. Like Sharp, he had a powerful arm and could sting the first baseman's hand with his strong throws. He joined the Navy in 1954 and served four years. After being discharged, he married Lolita Tschabold of Durand in 1959. He worked on Joe Gaffney's farm for seven years until he joined the Winnebago County Sheriff's Department in 1966, where he stayed until 1991. He then worked part-time in the U.S. Marshal Service and retired in 2005. Ditzler, who'll be 83 years old in November, and his wife live in Durand and had three children — Linda (who died in 2009), Lisa and Kurt — and two grandchildren.

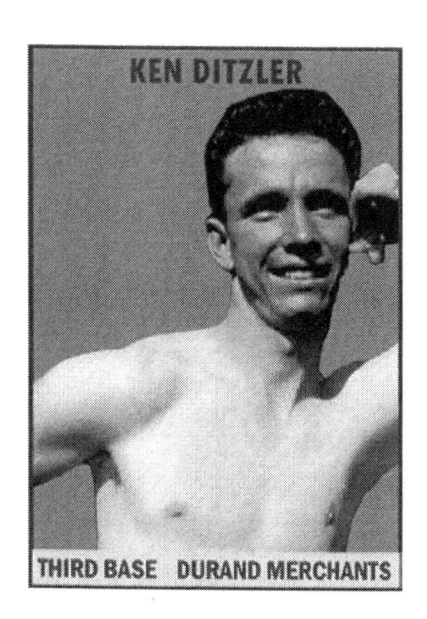

BILL ALBERSTETT

Bill Alberstett joined the Merchants after graduating from Durand High School in 1954 and was a very good hitter and first baseman. Though the Gazette failed to cover nine of the 29 games that year, the record shows that Alberstett was the team's leading hitter. It's unclear how many years he played with the Merchants. He was born Jan. 16, 1937, and farmed most of his life in the Durand and Pecatonica area until he retired and went to work for Rockford Blacktop. He married Shirley Keller on Sept. 14, 1956, and they had six children — Kristin, Kelly, Michael, Jaime, Mark and Joe — and 14 grandchildren. He was a veteran of the Navy reserves, a member and past president of the Durand School Board, a member of the Durand Athletic Association and, like Jerry Mulvain, an avid Cubs fan. He died on June 14, 2004 at age 67 after a sudden illness.

CHUCK TRACY

Chuck Tracy managed the Merchants from their first full season in 1949 until 1952, when Lloyd Mulvain became the player-manager. Tracy was born on April 23, 1907, in Marengo, Ill., and attended Rockford schools. He moved to Durand in 1941. He was a sheet metal worker for Mutimer Tin Shop in Rockford for 40 years and for 20 years was co-owner with his brother, Clifford "Tip" Tracy, of Tracys' Tin Shop in Durand. He worked for Taxon Heating in Rockford until his retirement. Tracy was an avid fisherman and hunter and played semi-pro baseball for many years. He was a terrific bowler and, with Merchant left fielder Fred Geiser, was among the first bowlers to be inducted into the Durand Bowling Association's Hall of Fame. He married Dorothy Whisman on April 20, 1926, in Rockford and they had five daughters—Shirley, Barbara, Sally, Karen and Susan — two sons — Wayne and Gary — 11 grandchildren and 13 great-grandchildren. He died at age 89 after a short illness on Nov. 30, 1996, in his Durand home.

CHARLES "BUZZ" STAUFFER

Reporter Buzz Stauffer covered the Merchants for the weekly Durand Gazette from 1949 to 1955. He arrived in Durand in 1947, leaving a job in a print shop in El Paso, Tex. He was born Oct. 4, 1923, in Susanville, Calif., moved to and graduated from high school in South Dakota and enrolled at Pennsylvania State University. He then enlisted in the Army and was assigned to specialized training programs at the University of Wisconsin and Michigan State University. A bachelor all the time he was in Durand, he rented a room at the home of Charlotte Heide on East Main Street. He was elected town clerk in 1953. After several disputes with Gazette owner John R. Van Sickle, who wanted more space devoted to community news and less devoted to the Merchants' games, Stauffer quit and moved to Montana, where he took a job with the Sidney Herald. In 1957, he joined The Dillon Daily Tribune staff and later edited the weekly Dillon Examiner for two years before returning to the Tribune as managing editor when the two papers merged in 1962. He married Evelyn Mikkelsen in 1958. In 1968, he was named the information director of Western Montana

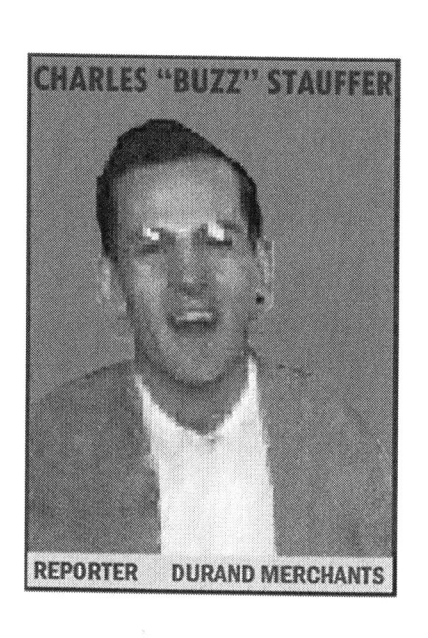

College in Dillon, where he remained until he retired more than 25 years later. His duties embraced several assignments, including publicity and publications, recruiting, fund-raising, alumni activities and 19 years as executive secretary of the Western Montana College Booster Club. He played a key role in saving the college from closure during hearings assessing a reorganization of the state college system in the 1970s. After retirement, he was honored by the Council for Advancement and Support of Education in Region 8 in the Northwestern United States and Western Canada with an Excellence Award presented in Coeur d'Alene, Idaho. He loved playing bridge — he was twice city champion with his partner Terry Cypher — and fishing the famed Beaverhead and Big Hole rivers. He and his wife were honored for their long-standing support of the school's athletic teams in 1996 when the college dedicated the Stauffer Conference Room in the physical education complex. Both Stauffer and his wife, who had no children, were elected to the Western Montana College Hall of Fame. He died after a long illness at age 75 on Nov. 20, 1998, in Barrett Memorial Hospital.

EARL "PETE" ADLEMAN

Pete Adleman was truly a jack-of-all trades but performed none of his jobs better than calling balls and strikes as home plate umpire for several years at nearly all softball or baseball games played at Legion Field. Roy Wilke and Jerry Mulvain loved him as an umpire because he was good and he was fair. When they thought Pete had missed a call, they never protested, they simply smiled at each other.

Adleman, born Dec. 2, 1903, served in the Army and was discharged in 1921. He married Gladys Wheeler on Oct. 10, 1928, and they had two daughters, June and

Shirley, Durand's greatest woman athlete in the 1950s and 1960s, four granddaughters and six great-grandchildren.

He built in 1943 and for three years operated the first Durand bowling alley. A terrific bowler himself, he was elected to the Durand Bowling Association's Hall of Fame. For several years, he was a distributor for Pinehurst Milk and for 20 years drove a Durand school bus. At one time he owned and operated at television repair business. He was a member of the Durand Methodist Church and for more than 60 years a member of the Durand Masonic Lodge No. 302. He was a member of the village board, superintendent of the village water works and road commissioner for Durand Township. He lived in Durand until 1968, when he and Gladys moved to Pearce, Ariz., to manage the Sunsites Trailer Court. In 1977, they moved to Willcox, Ariz., to manage the Grande Vista Trailer Court. After Gladys died in 1987, he moved to the Illinois Masonic Home in Sullivan in 1990. He died at age 88 at Decatur (Ill.) Memorial Hospital.

JOHN R. VAN SICKLE

John R. Van Sickle, born March 28, 1910, grew up in Durand. He graduated with a journalism degree from the University of Illinois in 1931 and purchased the weekly Durand Gazette when he couldn't find a job during the Depression. He expanded the business and eventually published weekly papers in the area towns of Davis, Rockton, Orangeville, Winslow, German Valley, Stillman Valley, Byron, Leaf River, Kirkland and Winnebago. As editor and publisher, he wrote a weekly column on the front page that commented mainly on national, international and religious issues. In 1942, he donated his old handfed press to the war effort, writing that "it's 2 ½ tons of scrap metal that may turn up in Tokyo or Berlin." He served on various governing bodies of the Methodist Church, first from Durand and then from Grace Church in Rockford, which included on five different general commissions of the national church as well as on the board of Garrett Theological Seminary.

He married another University of Illinois graduate, Mary Kathryn

Babcock, in Freeport on June 14, 1935, and they had two sons, John B. and Paul, and three grandchildren. Kathryn was organist and choir director of the Durand Methodist Church until they moved to Rockford in 1948 so their children could attend city schools. From 1962 to 1972, he was the first president of the board of trustees of the newly organized Wesley Willows Retirement Home in Rockford. After 43 years in the newspaper business, Van Sickle sold his Associated Publishers — which by now was partly owned by Frank Ryan, a Gazette printer who had married Lloyd Mulvain's widow — to Frank A. Wood Jr. of Denmark, Wis., near Green Bay. Seven years later, Van Sickle and his wife moved to Wesley Willows, where they lived until he died at age 94 on April 18, 2004, and she died at age 100 on Dec. 23, 2005.

THOMAS H. "DOC" YOUNG

Doc Young, born Oct. 14, 1888, was Durand's dentist from his graduation from Chicago Dental School in 1910 to 1964, and the town's patron saint of civic affairs. If it needing doing, chances are that Doc did it. He led efforts to create the first fire protection district in the state of Illinois, Durand's first volunteer fire department, the building of the town's first water system to protect it from fires, the construction of Legion Field, the paving of the Center Street town square and the organizing of the first Scout troops in Durand. He served in the Army Medical Corps during World War I and was a 50-year member of American Legion Gold Star Post No 676 and of Durand's Masonic Lodge No. 302. He also was a member of the Veterans of Foreign Wars and Veterans of World War I, Rockford Barracks 48. He served for 25 years on the Winnebago County Selective Service Board. His first marriage, which produced three children but only one, Betty, who survived to adulthood, ended in divorce. He then married Emogene Dailey, the widow of Harry Dailey, who was killed in his 20s in a highway accident in the early 1930s when he was hauling gasoline in a truck. Emogene had two sons, Dick and Ron. Doc retired from his dental practice in 1964 and moved to Rockford, where he died after a long illness at age 84 on Dec. 3, 1972, in the Americana Nursing Home.

BILL "THE BARBER" STEWARD

Bill Steward operated the Durand Barber Shop on the town square from 1947 until he retired in 1979. He was born May 17, 1917, grew up in Owen Center, Ill., and arrived in Durand in 1947. He bought the barber shop a couple of years later from Ellis Andrews, who owned and operated it for 31 years. Before that, the building, next to the Masonic Temple, was the home of Burton's Harness Shop. Steward was an Army veteran and served during World War II in Germany, where he purposely wrecked a Jeep he was driving to avoid hitting a German girl. He wound up with the Jeep's windshield on top of his chest and a severely injured right arm. He was laid up for nine months and eventually lost the use of about 20 percent of his arm. After his discharge, he attended the newly opened Decatur Barber School in Central Illinois.

During Steward's tenure, the barber shop served as the primary hangout for boys aged 7 to 70 where the main topics were the Merchants and major league baseball. The shop was the only place in town you could read The Sporting News, the weekly Bible of major league baseball (at that time no cable TV or ESPN existed and no daily newspaper printed all the baseball box scores — only The Sporting News published them).

Bill was a rapid Braves (and later Cubs) and Merchants fan. He loved pranks. Nearly every morning at 6:30 he would wait inside the back screen door of his home for Jack Walsh to deliver The Rockford Morning Star. When Jack got close to the door to toss the paper inside, Bill would let out a scream. "I knew it was coming, but it always scared me anyway," Jack recalls.

Bill was an avid hunter and after bagging a large buck one year organized a venison dinner to benefit our Little League team. More than 100 people paid $1.50 to attend the feed at the Grange Hall. For years afterward, the stuffed head of the buck decorated the wall of the barber shop.

On Aug. 14, 1949, he married Arlene Fosler. Four years later they moved into a new home three houses east of ours on East Main Street that had been built by Arlene's father, Oscar "Curley" Fosler, who had helped my dad renovate our home a couple of years earlier. After his retirement, Steward volunteered full time in his position as service officer for American Legion Gold Star Post No. 676, of which he was a member for more than 70 years. As the service officer, his duties included helping ailing veterans deal with hospitals and medical care and with various issues with the Department of Veteran Affairs. He built an 8-foot by 40-foot shed behind his house to store hospital and medical equipment that he and the Legion loaned out free to patients. For 43 years, from 1966 when the American Legion Post installed a flag pole in town square until 2009, Bill was the keeper of the flag, raising and lowering it each day. "I like to brag that I've really moved up in the world," Bill once told The Durand Gazette. "When I was in first grade, they handed me the flag and said I could be in charge of it. Fifty-six years later they handed me the flag and told me I was the flag custodian. That's advancement in life." For years, Bill, his wife Arlene and several Legion volunteers also placed flags around the village on holidays and put more than 400 flags on the graves of veterans in 11 cemeteries on each Memorial Day.

Bill died at home on March 10, 2015 at age 97. Survivors included his wife, three sons — Keith, Kim and Kerry — six grandchildren, four great grandchildren and a brother, Carl.

LEGION FIELD

Legion Memorial Field, the home of the Merchants since its construction at Dayton and East Elm streets by dozens of volunteers in 1948, is still the main venue for summer entertainment in Durand. Although many more bleacher seats have been added, it looks much the same today as it did nearly 70 years ago — the concession stand is simply a bigger version of the one where I turned in foul balls — and continues to host youth and adult softball and baseball games nearly every night. In addition, it is one of the home fields of the Durand-Pecatonica High School football team and draws large crowds during the fall for Friday night games.

TRASK BRIDGE PICNIC

The annual Trask Bridge Picnic was founded in 1911 by the Burritt Grange of Winnebago County, itself only two years old. Hailed as the "world's largest farm picnic," the event drew thousands of people to farmland adjacent to the Pecatonica River about five miles west of Durand. Events included baseball and softball games, exhibits of tractors, grain, poultry and bakery goods, coon house races and contests in log chopping, bundle tying, fly casting, hog calling and husband calling. By 1928, the picnic drew more than 50,000 people; attendance was approaching 60,000 after World War II. But losses in the Burritt Grange's membership and steadily declining attendance led to the picnic's demise in 1966.

THE CONTRIBUTORS TO "THE AGE OF INNOCENCE"

Shirley Adleman, 76, the daughter of Pete and Gladys Adleman, was a terrific athlete and spent much of her childhood playing sports with us boys because there were few opportunities for women athletes in the 1950s. She graduated from Durand High School in 1960 and moved to Alton, Ill., in 1967 and later to Cedar Hill, Mo. She now lives in Wood River, Ill. Like her dad, she was a school bus driver. Her riders were special education students to whom she devoted most of her time.

Mike Mulvain, 76, the younger son of Lloyd and Clara Lou Mulvain, was a terrific baseball catcher and hitter as well as a good basketball guard and football player. He graduated from Durand High School in 1960 and worked 29 years in Rockford for the Weyerhauser Paper Co. For the last 27 years, he and his wife, Pat, have owned and operated Mulvain Woodworks, a company a mile north of Durand that designs, manufacturers and installs various finished wood products. Mulvain had two sons by an earlier marriage and has two grandchildren.

Jim Walsh, 76, another member of the Durand High School Class of 1960, was a very good basketball player. He attended the Milwaukee School of Engineering and eventually joined the Illinois Bell Telephone Co. working in Joliet, Springfield, Aurora and Chicago before retiring after 30 years in 1991. After that, he did volunteer work for St. Mary's

Catholic Church and Medina Nursing Home in Durand and now spends much of his time installing furnaces and air conditioning systems in the area. He and his wife, Cheryl, have two daughters.

Bill Haggerty, like Mulvain and Walsh a buddy throughout our coming-of-age years in Durand, was an excellent second baseman and hitter on our baseball teams as well as a good basketball guard and football halfback. He also starred on the track team as a sprinter in the 100-yard and 220-yard dashes. He graduated from Durand High School with me in 1959 and four years later graduated from the University of Illinois in Champaign-Urbana. He then earned a Master's of Business Administration degree at Northern Illinois University in De Kalb. He worked for nearly 25 years for the Chicago & North Western Railroad and later for some other railroad companies. He retired in March 2007. Bill died at age 72 on March 29, 2014, at his home in Iowa City, Ia., after a lengthy battle with lung cancer.

Don Waller, my cousin who lived across the alley behind us and across the street from the water tower, didn't play on sports teams but with me, Mulvain, Walsh and Haggerty was a regular member of the Foul Ball Brigade at the Merchants' games. He graduated from Durand High School in 1956 and worked in Rockford at a fastener company even after he was stricken with muscular sclerosis in 1972. He and his wife, Sally, have fought a courageous and inspiring battle against the disease ever since. He kept working for a few years — sometimes rising at 4 a.m. to have enough time to get ready to be picked up by friends and driven to his Rockford job — even as the disease progressively worsened. When he lost all mobility, Sally used a hydraulic lift to get him in and out of bed. Eventually, he became totally paralyzed from the neck down. Sally no longer could take care of Don and moved him in 2003 to the Medina Nursing Home in Durand, where he died at age 71 in November 2009.

Mo Ostergard, 76, another baseball buddy who was an outstanding pitcher, also was a good basketball and football player. He graduated from Durand High School in 1960 and from Western Illinois University in Macomb in 1966. He taught three years at a high school in Van Nuys,

Calif., before trying his hand at sales, mostly in the construction trades. He then attended an electronics school and spent the next 25 years working in the radiology departments of various hospitals around the country. He spent the last seven years of his career at Kodak. He now lives in Davis, four miles west of Durand, and has one son.

The Dickerson brothers, Steve, 78, and John, 77, were good athletes. Steve was a star sprinter on the track team and John was a very good baseball, basketball and football player. Steve graduated from Durand High School in 1958 and John with my class in 1959. In 1962, Steve graduated with a mechanical engineering degree from the Illinois Institute of Technology in Chicago. He earned his master's degree in mechanical engineering the next year from the University of California at Berkeley and his doctor of science degree at the Massachusetts Institute of Technology in Cambridge. John graduated in 1963 with a degree in mechanical engineering at the Illinois Institute of Technology. He then earned his master's and doctor's degrees in applied mechanics at the California Institute of Technology in Pasadena. Steve was an assistant, associate and full professor of engineering from 1965 to 1996 at Georgia Tech University in Atlanta, where he was involved in starting up four companies. John was an assistant professor of mechanical engineering at the University of Texas in Austin from 1967 to 1974. He then spent the next 31 years as an associate professor of civil engineering at the University of South Carolina in Columbia, retiring in 2006. Another younger brother, Mark, also has a doctorate degree, in law, from Harvard University, and the two other brothers, Jim and Gregg, have bachelor of science degrees from Georgia Tech and the University of Georgia, respectively. Steve and his wife — Jane, who is the sister of Jim Walsh — now live in Atlanta where Steve is involved in two of his start-up businesses. They have two daughters and four grandchildren. John and his wife, Sandy, live in West Columbia, S.C., and have two sons and four grandsons.

Acknowledgements

Writing a book, like playing softball, is a team effort. I am grateful to dozens of teammates who assisted me in this effort.

First and foremost is Sherry McKenna Meinert, who writes the "Not So Long Ago..." column in the weekly Durand newspaper, The Volunteer. She did much of the research, tracked down several photographs, and served as an editor focusing on Durand history. Sherry, who lives on a small farm near Davis, Ill., and is a mother of three sons, was a bulldog at finding missing information. Had she chosen a career in journalism, the Durand native would have been a great reporter.

Sherry McKenna Meinert

The other two editors — Steve Proctor, deputy managing editor of The San Francisco Chronicle, and Karen Stabley, my former executive assistant at The Baltimore Sun — did a marvelous job of suggesting changes and spotting errors. Their work immensely improved the book. I also owe a great deal of gratitude to the three living members of the first Merchants' team of 1949 — Jerry Mulvain, Wayne Adleman and Fred Geiser. They were always generous with their time during their many hours of interviews with me. Other former Merchants who were always helpful no matter how often I interviewed them are Roger Sarver, Bernie Figi and Ken Ditzler.

I owe special thanks to Baltimore artist Katie Chrzanowski, who did a magnificent job of designing the Merchants' baseball cards appearing in Chapter 10.

I am profoundly grateful to Mike Mulvain, a Durand baseball boyhood buddy who now owns and operates Mulvain Woodworks a mile north of town. He was always available when a question needed answering and, with his wife Pat, constantly encouraging. He also was among the contributors to Chapter 6, recalling his experiences of growing up in Durand in the 1940s and 1950s.

Others who did a terrific job of writing about their childhood memories of Durand are Shirley Adleman, Jim Walsh, Mo Ostergard, Bill Haggerty, Don Waller, Steve Dickerson and John Dickerson.

Many of the photographs were contributed by Dave Mulvain, Dennis Bliss and Judy Wilke, widow of Roy Wilke. My older brother, Dave Waller, did a great job of scanning several photographs and sending them via email to me. My younger brother, Steve Waller, offered a superb description of Wilke's pitching style.

Also generous with their time were Bill and Arlene Steward, who were always just a phone call away when I needed information, and Lorraine Vormezeele, who provided me with the letter her mother, Anne Walsh, wrote to her grandchildren about the Walsh family's battle with polio.

Others who assisted included Bob Haggerty, Bob Adleman, Steve Battern, Jim and Sharon Place, Mary Jo Hubbardtt, Sid Felder, Sally Kelsey Lawson, Pat Smith Albrecht, Judy Smith Osborne, June Adleman Hardesty, Dick and Sally Cuthbertson, Carla Vendel, Gary Raetz, Gary Nuss, Norm Chilton, Ken Greene and the Otter Creek Historical Society.

Also helping were Ed Mahoney of The Hartford Courant, Dianne Donovan of The Baltimore Sun, Mary Holt of the Dillon (Mont.) Public Library, The Dillon Tribune, Charlotte Hall of The Orlando Sentinel, Marty Petty of The St. Petersburg Times and Kevin Kallaugher, former cartoonist of The Baltimore Sun.

My thanks also go to Al McCartney, Maxine McCartney, Sally Waller, Beverly Waller, Frances Waller, Bobby Highland, Marcia Highland, Kate Hartman, Julie Sharp, Janet Stringer, Amy Stringer, Barbara Smith, Kevin Steward, Jack Walsh, Jim Spelman, Dan McCullough, Helen C. Johnson, Joyce Long, Richard Jones, George Dilli, Bill Flynn, Jeff Marx, John Jenkins, Jane Dystel, Tony Schlegel and Ian Harries.

I am especially grateful to Monroe Dodd, formerly of The Kansas City Star and Times, who shepherded the first edition of this book through the production process, and his wife, Jean Dodd, who worked her magic in designing the book and its magnificent cover.

Last but not least, I owe special thanks to my wife, Donna, who was always supportive and served as another editor, spotting errors and offering excellent suggestions.

Acknowledgements II

Once again I owe a great deal of gratitude to Sherry Meinert, the former columnist for The Volunteer, who was always ready to look up the latest piece of information I needed for the second edition of Durand's Marvelous Merchants.

I'm also grateful to Jim Spelman, Jim Walsh, Mo Ostergard and Mike Mulvain, who recalled many more delightful tales of growing up in Durand in the 1940s and 1950s that hadn't been included in the earlier version of the book.

Many thanks, too, to my brothers and sister, Dave Waller, Steve Waller and Martha Young, and cousin Jim Place, who remembered more of life from the past. Also contributing were Jack Walsh, Ken Waller, Ed Larson, Dan Highland — son of Merchants' first baseman Dick Highland — Donna Koglin Ackerman, Marcia Koglin Peyton, Maryellyn Lilley Kinney and Neva Wallace Gunz.

Special thanks go to Jean Dodd, who designed and produced both versions of Durand's Marvelous Merchants.

Notes

All accounts of Durand Merchants' softball games, except if otherwise noted, came from stories in the weekly Durand Gazette. Sources who are identified in the text are not included in these notes.

Chapter 1 Build It, But Will They Come?

13 "They were members…" Tom Brokaw, The Greatest Generation, p. vii, preface.
13 "Of 171 Durand boys…" Traveling Through Time: A Historical Look at Durand's 150 years, p. 6.
13 "Catcher Jerry Mulvain joined the Marines…and Brother Lloyd…" Interview with Jerry Mulvain, Jan. 31, 2007.
13 "Shortstop Lloyd Mulvain…" Ibid.
13 "Second baseman Bob Highland…" The Volunteer, Oct. 15, 1998.
14 "Third baseman Wayne Adleman…" Interview with Wayne Adleman, Jan. 4, 2007.
14 "Left fielder Fred Geiser…joined the Navy Seabees…" Interview with Fred Geiser, May 9, 2007.
14 "Right fielder Keith 'Bud' Smith…was in the Army Transportation Corps…" Durand Gazette, Oct. 25, 1990.
14 "Right fielder George Smith…" The Volunteer, Oct. 22, 1998.
14 "Outfielder Wayne 'Red' Barron…" The Volunteer, June 25, 1992.

15 "From 1946...some of them played on the Durand town team..." Various editions of the Durand Gazette, 1946 and 1948.
15 "Teams from all over Northern Illinois..." Gary Raetz, Rock Run County Historical Society news letter published in The Volunteer, Feb. 12, 1998.
15 "The diamond was constructed..." Ibid.
16 "The ballpark campaign was led..." Interview with Bill Steward, Feb. 2, 2007.
17 "He organized the first Scout troop..." Durand Gazette, Dec. 7, 1972.
17 "In the early 20th Century...a fire that started in the Geary Restaurant..." Traveling Through Time, p. 89.
17 "Thirteen years later, fires..." Ibid., p. 90.
17 "Doc Young came to the rescue. He organized..." Freeport Journal- Standard, March 17, 1960.
18 "Local response was mostly favorable..." Ibid. 184.
18 "Doc became the new department's..." Traveling Through Time, p. 12 and p. 90 and Changing Ways, published by the Durand Bicentennial Committee, p. 51.
18 "They had plenty of help...Keller then donated the property to the Legion." Durand Gazette, April 15, 1948.
18 "Carl Holland...job of clearing the land." Interview with Karen Holland Reddy, Dec. 14, 2014.
18 "The house was condemned and volunteers..." Interviews with Jerry Mulvain, Jan. 31, 2007; Roger Sarver, Feb. 3, 2007; and Fred Geiser, May 9, 2007.
19 "Those that couldn't be bulldozed..." Letter from Dave Mulvain, April 11, 2007.
19 "The Charge of the Light Brigade was led..." Ibid. and interview with Jerry Mulvain, Jan. 31, 2007.
19 "A three-day local carnival...24 1,500-watt lights." The Durand Gazette, June 24, 1948.
19 "Amundsen, who got the lights..." Interview with Fred Geiser, May 9, 2007, and letter from Dave Mulvain, April 11, 2007.
22 "What the story didn't mention..." Interview with Jerry Mulvain, Jan. 31, 2007.
23 "Several businesses...sponsored the team...the businesses included..." addresses and histories from Gary Raetz for Chilton Realty calendars, from Helen C. Johnson records and from The Durand Gazette and Rockford Morning News.
27 "The year's biggest news..." Melinda Corey, Chronology of 20th -Century America, p. 60.
27 "The Chicago Cubs..." Jerome Holtzman and George Vass, The Chicago Cubs Encyclopedia, p. 89.
28 "The Rockford Peaches..." Website (aagpbl.org) of the All-American Girls Professional Baseball League and The New York Times.

Chapter 2 The Greatest Season

35 "Nobody goes there anymore..." Yogi Berra, The Yogi Book, p. 16.
35 "Earl 'Pete' Adleman...would park his car..." Interview with Jerry Mulvain, Jan.

31, 2007.
36   "Nearly every Sunday night Edward and Edna Meier..." email from Beverly Waller, July 24, 2007.
36   "On Sunday afternoons, George Smith..." Interview with Jerry Mulvain, Jan. 31, 2007, and June 10, 2007.
36   "Lloyd Mulvain discovered an out-building..." Interview with Jerry Mulvain, Jan. 31, 2007.
42   "McMahon probably could have beaten Hines..." Interview with Roger Sarver, Feb. 3, 2007.
43   "President Truman presented to Congress..." Corey, Chronology of 20th-Century America, p. 61.
43   "Leo Durocher, manager of the New York Giants..." Holtzman and Vass, The Chicago Cubs Encyclopedia, p. 71.
43   "The New York Yankees of Joe DiMaggio..." The Baseball Encyclopedia, p. 2674.
44   "The Rockford Peaches continued to make history..." Website (aagbpl.org) of the All-American Girls Professional Baseball League.

Chapter 3 John R. Van Sickle's Durand Gazette

Except where otherwise noted, the account of John R. Van Sickle's years at the Durand Gazette came from his book In This Column, published in 1980.

56   "Much of the Gazette's news read like the writings of the Duke of Paducah..." Traveling Through Time, p. 40.
61   "Within two years all but the sewer system..." Ibid., p. 91.
61   "Completing the sewer system..." Ibid., p. 92.

Chapter 4 Running Out of Adjectives

64   "During a typical week, he played three nights..." Interview with Jerry Mulvain, Jan. 31, 2007.
64   "Lloyd also played baseball..." Interview with Wayne Adleman, Jan. 4, 2007.
68   "Wilke had come by this pitching style..." Interview with Roger Sarver, June 9, 2007.
68   "Among the several pitchers in the region..." Interviews with Jerry Mulvain, Jan. 31, 2007, and Wayne Adleman, Jan. 4, 2007.
68   "Kirk...was recruited by the Henney Hearse Co...." Freeport Journal-Standard, May 28, 2007.
69   "Feigner...won more than 10,000 games..." Website of kingandhiscourt.com.
69   "Sterkle led the Sealmasters..." Website (softball.org/halloffame) of the Amateur Softball Association of America.
78   "Just five years earlier, in 1945..." Traveling Through Time, p. 91.
79   "The year was marked by the beginning of the Korean War..." Corey, Chronology of 20th-Century America, p. 62-63.
79   "In baseball, the Cubs..." Holtzman and Vass, The Chicago Cubs Encyclopedia, p. 72.

79 "The New York Yankees..." The Baseball Encyclopedia, p. 2675.
79 "The Rockford Peaches won..." Website (aagpbl.org) of the All-American Girls Professional Baseball League.

Chapter 5 A Lost Season

89 "McMahon...moved in 1950 to Corpus Christi..." Durand Gazette, June 7, 1951.
89 "Adleman was an infielder and...wound up playing..." email from Bob Adleman, March 26, 2007.
89 "He was the kind of player who would announce..." Interview with Roger Sarver, Feb. 3, 2007.
89 "He signed a contract with the Corpus Christi Aces..." Durand Gazette, June 7, 1951.
95 "He joined the Durand Post Office in 1936..." The Volunteer, Nov. 23, 2006.
95 "Bump...retired after 46 years..." Rockford Register Star, March 19, 1994.
95 "Dad delivered mail to 235 customers..." The Volunteer, Nov. 23, 2006.
95 "He was a charter member of the Durand Lions Club...and the village clerk from 1971 to 1977..." The Volunteer, March 4, 1999.
95 "The first Citizens of the Year..." Traveling Through Time, p. 38.
96 "The year was marked by the election of Republicans..." Corey, Chronology of 20th-Century America, p. 64.
97 "In baseball, the Cubs posted..." Holtzman and Vass, The Chicago Cubs Encyclopedia p. 73.
97 "The New York Yankees, paced by sluggers..." The Baseball Encyclopedia, p. 2676.
97 "The Rockford Peaches won..." Website (aagpbl.org) of the All-American Girls Professional Baseball League.

Chapter 6 The Age of Innocence

101 "The outdoor free show, which was started in 1937..." Durand Gazette, May 6, 1937.
105 "It was invented in the 1930s...by the end of 1949 there were two million TV sets..." Charles A. Wills, America in the 1940s, p. 115-116.
106 "Bill's dad, Frank 'Ted' Haggerty, won the set...the reception from the Davenport station..." Interview with Bob Haggerty, April 15, 2007.
106 "Clear reception didn't arrive until 1953..." Website (wtvo.com) of WTVO in Rockford.
107 "Nuns from Chicago, including Sister Euchrista..." Interview with Dave Waller, Sept. 11, 2007.
107 "Father Driscoll was pitching to Bill Flynn..." Interview with Bob Haggerty, Sept. 10, 2007.
108 "Most of it came from the crates..." Interview with Dave Waller, Sept. 11, 2007.

Chapter 7 Wilke's Swan Song

131 "Running unopposed in the town elections..." Durand Gazette, April 23, 1953.

134 **"Reporter Stauffer and owner John R. Van Sickle had a long-standing dispute..."** Interviews with Wayne Adleman, Jan. 4, 2007, and Fred Geiser, May 9, 2007.

135 **"Jerry Mulvain's young daughters..."** Interview with Jerry Mulvain, Jan. 31, 2007.

135 **"Bernie Figi's young son..."** Interview with Jerry and Juanita Mulvain, June 10, 2007.

140 **"The biggest local news of the year was...Pfc. Charles H. Long...declared missing in action..."** The Volunteer, Nov. 2, 2006.

140 **"A year later the War Department...Long's remains were sent back to Durand..."** Ibid.

140 **"On July 27, representatives of the United Nations..."** Corey, Chronology of 20th-Century America, p. 65.

140 **"The Braves, led by slugger Eddie Mathews..."** The Baseball Encyclopedia, p. 351.

140 **"Even the addition of slugger Ralph Kiner..."** Holtzman and Vass, The Chicago Cubs Encyclopedia, p. 75.

141 **"The New York Yankees won their fifth straight..."** The Baseball Encyclopedia, p. 2678.

141 **"The Rockford Peaches finished in fourth place..."** Website (aagpbl.org) of the All-American Girls Professional Baseball League.

Chapter 8 Slow Start, Fast Finish

143 **"Winnebago and the Merchants had played at least six times since 1949..."** Various stories in the Durand Gazette from 1949 to 1953.

143 **"Stringer was known as 'Mr. Change Up'..."** Rockford Register Star, June 29, 1994.

143 **"He was a veteran...and his family was among the original settlers..."** Ibid.

151 **"Dr. Jonas Salk, developer of the Salk vaccine..."** Corey, Chronology of 20th-Century America, p. 65.

151 **"The Army-McCarthy hearings..."** Ibid., p. 65-66. 6   **"The Supreme Court tackled the race question..."** Ibid., p. 66.

151 **"In baseball, the Cleveland Indians..."** The Baseball Encyclopedia, p. 2679.

151 **"The Milwaukee Braves, in their second season..."** Ibid., p. 355.

151 **"The Chicago Cubs, with Ernie Banks..."** Holtzman and Vass, The Chicago Cubs Encyclopedia, p. 76.

151 **"The Rockford Peaches, in the final year..."** Website (aagpbl.org) of the All-American Girls Professional Baseball League.

Chapter 9 Tragic Events

153 **"Pitcher Russ Stringer returned...and was joined by several rookies..."** Durand Gazette, June 23, 1955.

154 **"Others on the team were..."** Durand High School yearbook, 1959.

154 **"Others on the team were 6th man..."** Durand High School yearbook, 1962.

155 "The parish priest…said a special mass on Sept. 11…" Letter from Anne Walsh in the 1980s to her grandchildren.
156 "At about the same time, the parents…were approached…" Ibid.
156 "Not wanting to leave their ill children…the three of them flew…" Interview with Lorraine Vormezeele, Feb. 9, 2007.
156 "The show's host didn't ask Lorraine…so much mail arrived…more than $10,000…" Ibid.
167 "Keron Walsh died 20 years later…Anne Walsh died at age 76…" Ibid.

Chapter 10 Whatever Happened to Them?

174 "Roy was born…he joined the Hill Brothers…" The Volunteer, Sept. 8, 2005.
174 "Two years after leaving…Roy started his own company…" Ibid.
175 "He also loved cattle shows…and would take another of his nephews…" Interview with Jim Place, Feb. 19, 2007.
175 "He enjoyed boxing…" Ibid.
175 "He and his wife Judy were members…" The Volunteer, Sept. 8, 2005.
176 "Roy married my mother's half-sister, Betty Amundsen…" Ibid.
177 "Betty died of heart disease…" Freeport Journal-Standard, Jan. 10, 1983.
177 "A year later, Roy married Beverly Geiser…" The Volunteer, Sept. 8, 2005.
177 "She died three years later at age 54…slightly more than a year later…Roy married Judy Schulte…" Ibid.
177 "In 2001, Roy had a bout with bladder cancer…he predicted that cancer… would come back…" Interview with Judy Wilke, June 12, 2007.
177 "Severe liver cancer…Roy replied in his drawl…" Ibid.

JERRY MULVAIN: Information about Jerry Mulvain's life came from interviews with him on Jan. 31, 2007, May 4, 2007 and June 10, 2007; with Wayne Adleman on Jan. 4, 2007; and with Roger Sarver on Feb. 3, 2007.

LLOYD MULVAIN: Information about Lloyd Mulvain's life came from interviews with Jerry Mulvain on Jan. 31, 2007, with Mike Mulvain on June 11, 2007, and from The Rockford Morning Star, April 3, 1956.

WAYNE ADLEMAN: Information on Adleman's life came from interviews with him on Jan. 4, 2007, and Aug. 28, 2007, and with Jerry Mulvain on June 10, 2007.

JACK SHARP: Information of Sharp's life came from The Rockford Morning Star, June 6, 1988.

DICK HIGHLAND: Information on Dick Highland's life came from The Durand Gazette, Jan 27, 1977.

BOB HIGHLAND: Information on Bob Highland's life came from an interview with Jerry Mulvain on Jan. 31, 2007, and from The Volunteer, Oct. 15, 1998.

JOHN HARTMAN: Information on Hartman's life came from an email from Sherry McKenna Meinert on Sept. 9, 2007, and The Volunteer, Sept. 16, 2004.

FRED GEISER: Information on Geiser's life came from interviews with him on May 9, 2007, and with Jerry Mulvain on Jan. 31, 2007, and from an email from Sherry McKenna Meinert on Aug. 26, 2007.

JOE HINES: Information on Hines' life came from The Durand Gazette, July 19, 1990.

JACK YAUN: Information on Yaun's life came from The Janesville Gazette in Wisconsin, Oct. 21, 2006.

THE SMITH BROTHERS : Information on Keith "Bud" Smith's life came from The Durand Gazette, Oct. 25, 1990, and on George Smith's life from The Volunteer, Oct. 22, 1998.

WAYNE "RED" BARRON: Information on Barron's life came from The Volunteer, June 25, 1992.

BERNIE FIGI: Information on Figi's life came from interviews with him on Feb. 12, 2007, and from an email from Sherry McKenna Meinert, Sept. 9, 2007.

JOHNNIE SMITH: Information on Smith's life came from The Durand Gazette, April 26, 1984.

JACK MCMAHON: Information on McMahon's life came from an email from his niece, Carla Vendel, March 7, 2007.

DON HUBBARTT : Information on Hubbartt's life came from an interview with his wife, Mary Jo Hubbartt, on March 2, 2007, and from The Rockford Register Star, Oct. 9, 2000.

VERNAL JONES: Information on Jones' life came from The Independent- Register of Brodhead, Wis., March 4, 1982.

RUSS STRINGER: Information on Stringer's life came from The Rockford Register Star, June 29, 1994.

KEN DITZLER: Information on Ditzler's life came from an interview with him on May 6, 2007, and from an email from Sherry McKenna Meinert, Sept. 5, 2007.

BILL ALBERSTETT: Information on Alberstett's life came from The Volunteer, June 17, 2004, and from an email from Sherry McKenna Meinert, Aug. 16, 2007.

CHUCK TRACY: Information on Tracy's life came from The Volunteer, Dec. 5, 1996.

CHARLES "BUZZ" STAU FFER: Information on Stauffer's life came from The Dillon Tribune in Montana, Nov. 25, 1998.

EARL "PETE" ADLEMAN: Information on Adleman's life came from interviews with his daughter, Shirley, on Jan. 29, 2007, Feb. 2, 2007, and Aug. 27, 2007.

THE CONTRIBUTORS TO "THE AGE OF INNOCENCE:" Information on the lives of the contributors to Chapter 6 — Shirley Adleman, Mike Mulvain, Jim Walsh, Bill Haggerty, Don Waller, Mo Ostergard, Steve Dickerson and John Dickerson — came from interviews with and emails from them and an interview with Sally Waller, Sept. 9, 2007.

About the Author

Mike Waller at one of his favorite haunts, Churchill Downs, Louisville.

Mike Waller was born Sept. 7, 1941, and grew up in Durand, Ill. He watched scores of Durand Merchant softball games at Legion Field and chased foul balls among the parked cars, grabbing more than his share of them. He played baseball from age 10 to 17 on Durand teams in Little League, Pony League and an American Legion league. Waller also played baseball in high school, as well as basketball, football and track and field. He played basketball and baseball for two years at Millikin University in Decatur, Ill., before graduating in 1963.

Waller started his newspaper career in 1961 as a sports clerk and reporter at The Decatur Herald. He joined the copy editing staff of The Cleveland Plain Dealer in 1965 and moved to Louisville, Ky., in 1967, where he worked 11 years as a copy editor, chief of the copy desk, assistant managing editor and executive sports editor of The Courier-Journal and Louisville Times.

In 1978, he joined the staff of The Kansas City Star and became the only editor in The Star's history to serve in the top three newsroom positions: managing editor of The Star, managing editor of its sister paper, The Kansas City Times, and editor of The Kansas City Star and Times.

Waller was named executive editor of The Hartford Courant in 1986, became The Courant's editor in 1990 and was appointed publisher and chief executive officer of The Courant in 1994. Three years later he was named publisher and CEO of The Baltimore Sun and senior vice president of the Time Mirror Company. He retired from The Sun at the end of 2002 and now lives with his wife, Donna, on Hilton Head Island, SC., where he played an average of 312 rounds of golf a year until he started writing this book. He'll be lucky to get in 250 rounds in 2007. But, he confessed, writing "Durand's Marvelous Merchants" was as much fun as breaking 80 on the golf course.

During his 41-year career, he worked for newspapers that won dozens of national journalism awards, including eight Pulitzer Prizes. As a business executive in Hartford and Baltimore, Waller served on the board of directors of more than two dozen non-profit organizations. He was the chairman of two United Way campaigns, in Hartford and Baltimore, which raised a total of about $70 million.

Made in the USA
Columbia, SC
16 October 2018